'Charlie, Don't Be a Hero'

A Mother's Story of the Extraordinary Life of
Her Son, U.S. Navy SEAL Charles Keating IV

D1600249

Krista Keating-Joseph

Colonel (Retired) Will G. Merrill Jr.

'Charlie, Don't Be a Hero'
A Mother's Story of the Extraordinary Life
of Her Son, U.S. Navy SEAL Charles Keating IV

Copyright, 2020
Krista Keating-Joseph
Colonel (Retired) Will G. Merrill Jr.

No text or images in this book may be used or reproduced in any
manner without written permission from the publisher or authors.

All Rights Reserved
Interior Pages Layout by Capri Porter
Printed in the United States

ISBN: 978-1-7347007-3-2 (Hardcover)
ISBN: 978-1-7347007-4-9 (Paperback)

Published by Legacies & Memories
St. Augustine, Florida
www.LegaciesandMemoriesPublishing.com

Cover portrait courtesy of CJ Stafford (Portraits by CJ)

President Barack Obama's quote on the cover is an excerpt
from his Memorial Day speech May 30, 2016.

President Donald J. Trump's quote on the cover is an
excerpt from his April 17, 2018 letter to Krista
Keating-Joseph after reading Krista's book,
Big-Hearted Charlie Runs the Mile,
an inspirational children's book based
on her son, Charles Keating IV.

Quotes by Charles Keating IV in the Epigraph are
excerpted from his notecards used in a speech
December 23, 2015, at the Florida Department
of Environmental Protection Agency.

This book is a true account based on facts, documents and memories
of the authors, including Krista Keating-Joseph's recollections of stories
that were told to her by her son, Charles Keating IV. Dialogue of some
conversations in the book is not word-for-word.

Contact the Author, Krista Keating-Joseph
www.KristaKeatingJoseph.com
www.CharlieDontBeAHero.com

Dedication

To all parents who have lost a child.

Contents

Foreword

By Stephen M. Rasche

I had been working as part of the staff of the Chaldean Catholic Church in Northern Iraq for nearly two years when Charlie Keating IV was killed in a fierce battle with ISIS fighters in the town of Teleskof, an empty Christian town in the no-man's land between ISIS and coalition forces then entrenched south of Al Qosh. In their drive North in the summer of 2014, ISIS had been stopped just outside Al Qosh, the historic Christian town of the Chaldean Catholic Church, and it had been the remaining Christian outpost in Northern Nineveh still not taken.

As the news came to us in the Kurdistan Region capital of Erbil, some 60 miles to the East, I reflected in sadness about the death of another US service member. Mine was a military family, and these things were always close to home. Still, I knew nothing about Charlie Keating IV himself, and in the chaos of the war and displacement that we served in, my focus soon moved on, as it had to, to the other matters at hand - in our case tens of thousands of displaced Christians and other minorities struggling to hang on, who were under our protection and care.

Months later, while visiting in New York as the guest of the Archdiocese of New York, Cardinal Dolan mentioned having said Mass at St. Patrick's for the US Navy Seal who had been killed that Spring in Northern Iraq. I had not known until then that Charlie Keating IV had been Catholic, or even a person of faith for that matter. By then ISIS had been pushed back completely from Teleskof and the town, in its war damaged state, had been returned to the people, with the Church essentially the only functioning civil authority there. We knew the spot where Charlie had given his life, and the details of the battle that had taken place there, but nothing really about Charlie himself.

A week later, back in Iraq, I was with Fr. Salar, the Vicar

General of the Diocese of Al Qosh, who had been given the responsibility as well of rebuilding Teleskof and bringing about its return to life. I was assigned by the Church to assist him in this work, and was primarily responsible for finding funds and setting up programs for work. So began several months of traveling up and down the road daily where Charlie's last battle had taken place.

The battle had been intense. In a surprise attack on a lightly armed joint US-Kurdish advise and assist team, more than 120 ISIS fighters had rammed through perimeter lines in force. In the fourteen-hour battle that ensued 58 ISIS fighters were killed and over twenty of their vehicles destroyed, and by the end of the fight Teleskof had been cleared. As part of the fight, a Navy SEAL quick-reaction force had been sent in by land approaching from the North to save the coalition team, together with heavy air support from US F-15s, F-16s, A-10s and even B-52s. At 9:32 a.m., May 3, 2016, as part of that SEAL team, Special Warfare Operator 1st Class Charles "Chuck " Keating IV, was struck and killed by direct ISIS sniper fire.

The town was finally declared safe for return to its displaced Christian residents in early November of 2016. It would be months before power and water were fully returned, but the rebuilding work began in earnest, with Fr. Salar and the Church essentially now acting as construction managers. Eventually a reconstruction grant from the Hungarian Government to the Chaldean Church of over two million dollars would allow for the town to recover, but the heavily damaged buildings on the North end of the town would remain battle-scarred for more than two years.

In that time, Fr. Salar and I would drive through the battle site on a daily basis. We knew exactly the place on the road where Charlie had been when he was hit, and the building from which the sniper fire had come. I would pray silently as we passed that place, and often Fr. Salar and I would talk about the importance of someday building some sort of remembrance of all that had happened to the town, something that could also respectfully and permanently include the name and sacrifice of Charlie Keating.

In the summer of 2018, a visit by a high-level US government delegation to the region led to a discussion between representatives of Vice President Pence and Fr. Salar. Included in that discussion was the interest of private Americans in supporting some sort of remembrance on the ground for Charlie. Out of this discussion, I was put in contact with Charlie's family, including Krista Keating-Joseph, Charlie's mother and the author of this book.

In the time since, the Nineveh region of Iraq has remained simmering on the edge of additional fighting between all the competing power factions that still have designs on the area. Safety for the town of Teleskof has fluctuated, making long-term reconstruction efforts stunted and cautious. Still, when and if things return to stability, I have great confidence that a proper remembrance will be built there for Charlie. We pray for that day when Charlie's family and friends can come and see for themselves.

But in the end, I think, this book is not about the where and when of Charlie Keating's death. It is about the bond of a mother and child, and especially a military mother and child, and the central importance of their shared faith, and how it continues to live. In the ancient Christian town of Teleskof, in a country which received the gospel from the original apostles in the first Century A.D., the deep strength of the bond between mother Mary and child is ingrained into every fiber of their being. So it is with the story of mother and child in this book.

Stephen M. Rasche JD is Vice Chancellor of the Catholic University in Erbil where he is Director of the Institute of Ancient and Threatened Christianity. He also serves as Counsel to the Chaldean Catholic Archdiocese of Erbil. Throughout the course of the ISIS war in Iraq he served on the ground with the Church alongside its priests and lay leaders. He is the author of the book

The Disappearing People: The Tragic Fate of Christians in the Middle East, *Post Hill Press, 2020.*

Preface

When I first contacted Krista Keating-Joseph, I had thought that the heroism of her son, Charles Keating IV, would be an excellent story for a chapter of the book, *Ordinary People: Extraordinary Heroes- Afghanistan and Iraq,* that I was working on at the time.

In later discussions, it became obvious to both of us that the story of his heroism, death and life should be told in a book. We decided to work together on this story, and we did. I wrote, she edited. She wrote, I edited.

Over the next four years I watched as a grieving Gold Star mother came to the realization that her son's death was not in vain. I saw her as a strong, faithful woman who put her tears aside so she could tell the story of her son's bravery, his development as a young lad, his deep desire to become a Navy SEAL, followed by his deployments and, his last deployment in Iraq, where he died a heroic death.

Being a military man for much of my life, I have seen boys grow up and become men. When you look at a picture of a fallen soldier you don't realize the level of training, and the fact that earlier in their lives, they were just kids growing up in America. Yet, their faith and love of their country, combined with an adventurous spirit, resulted in them becoming soldiers, sailors and airmen proudly defending our great country.

Some of these men and women have made their service into careers. Many become senior enlisted, some become General officers. All are invariably proud of their service.

Many of those who I had the good fortune to meet and interview joined the military – not knowing what the future might hold. Charlie's decision to become a Navy SEAL after the attack on our nation on 9/11, likewise, was made not knowing what the future might bear. Yet, his patriotism, sense of adventure and love of his country were the factors that inspired his decision to leave college and serve our nation.

As you read this book, you will become assured that the future of our country is in good hands as long as we have people like Charles Keating IV serving to protect it!

It has been my privilege and honor to be able to help tell the stories of many genuine American heroes, their families, and their service to our country.

Will G. Merrill Jr., Colonel (Retired) U.S. Army

'Charlie, Don't Be a Hero'

A Mother's Story of the Extraordinary Life of
Her Son, U.S. Navy SEAL Charles Keating IV

"Be passionate about your job, no matter what it is. You'll always be respected if you are passionate...."

"...Every action affects the bigger picture."

U.S. Navy SEAL Charles Keating IV, December 23, 2015

PART I

'He's in Heaven, Mommy'

Prologue

Jan. 9, 2012

To my sister Ali,

This is your older brother Charlie. I remember the day you were born. I was 20 years old and in my freshman year of college at Indiana. I was so stoked to have another little sister. It was pretty funny because every time I saw you, you had the biggest smile on your face but nothing was funnier than seeing you upset. Also, going out in public everyone thought you were my kid, which was extremely awkward when Mom was around. I always think about how much you love the water, no matter how warm or cold it is. Just remember you have the greatest parents in the world and I've seen how much they care for you. Also, I hope you have worked on your phone and Skype skills since you were 7 because every time I try to talk to you it's No phone, bye Charlie! But I still love you. I could never be a prouder older brother. I keep a picture of you whenever I go on trips or overseas. I'm writing this letter in a village in Northern Afghanistan and hope you will never see this. Mom made me promise I'd write you one even though I insisted I'll be alright. I don't think these people (Taliban) like SEALS too much! Just remember with whatever happens to me I will always be with you and I'll be in a much happier place. Keep Mom and your Dad strong and keep your faith in God.

Love you lots

C4

Chapter 1

December 27, 2015

I nudged Charlie with my hand. "Can Brooke go to the car ahead of you so I can talk to you for a second?" I wanted one more moment alone with my son before his next deployment.

Brooke and I embraced. "It was great to meet you," I told her. "Stay in touch."

She walked toward their car, leaving us alone at the front door.

"Look, Charlie," I said, "watch your drinking. Be good with Brooke. Be thoughtful with her."

He nodded as I paused before giving him the advice my mother's intuition told me he needed to hear.

"You have this habit of risking your life to save people. Please … *don't be a hero.*"

As soon as this statement left my lips, I remembered the day Charlie told me "I barely survived, but saved some lives today because of my steeplechase training. I have been recommended for a Bronze Star Medal with a *V* for valor because of it."

I found out later, Charlie was behind a wall with other SEALs and with "partner forces" when he jumped over the wall under heavy fire, ran out and grabbed an injured Afghan interpreter and an American weapon that ISIS was about to capture. He ran back with them, jumped back over the wall, and got everyone into a safe location. It was definitely a steeplechase situation.

I repeated, "Please, Charlie. Don't be a hero."

Charlie flashed his infectious smile. I stared deep into those same stunning blue eyes that had drawn me in when I held my first baby in my arms.

"Don't worry," he assured me. "I'll be fine. I love you."

"I love you too."

I watched my son, carefree as ever, head down the sidewalk. I knew he'd turn and look back at me. He always did. After one more "I've got this" nod, he disappeared around the corner to the driveway.

But this send-off was different. This deployment felt different. I dashed out of the house and around the corner. Charlie was already in the driver's seat.

"Charlie," I called out, "I've got to hug you one more time!" My son stepped out of the car and gave me a tight, long hug before returning to his seat. Standing in the driveway I waved at both of them as the car backed into the cul-de-sac. "Goodbye," I said, unsure they could hear me. As Charlie and Brooke pulled away, I fixed my gaze on their rear window.

Please, I thought, *be looking back at me.*

I returned to the house and closed the front door. Through the glass, I could see Charlie's car down the street and I watched his taillights fade into the dawn.

I knew I'd never see my son again.

Chapter 2

May 1, 2016

"Hi, Mom!"

A Facetime call from Charlie during Sunday dinner preparation was a welcome, wonderful surprise.

"Hey, Charlie," I said, "what's going on?"

"Just wanted to call you."

"You doing okay?" I asked, slightly worried at why he wanted to talk to me.

Charlie had Facetimed us from Iraq six weeks earlier. He looked great then. He was freshly showered. He'd had his hair cut short before he left, but it had grown out and his beautiful feathered hair was flipped back like it was earlier, when he'd had time to style it. He was happy and healthy, his eyes dancing on my phone screen as he described how his team had blown up a large Trojan horse vehicle ISIS had attempted to use to sneak into a Kurdish Peshmerga-controlled village. Typical Charlie. He left out the details I later learned of his being the hero of that battle, earning the nickname "Rambo" among the Peshmerga fighters.

Charlie ended up receiving the Navy Cross (the highest Navy military award) because he: "Continually exposed himself to enemy automatic weapon, mortar and rocket-propelled grenade fire as he diligently maneuvered between the front and flanks of the defensive fighting position to stop enemy advances and keep friendly forces accurately informed of the unfolding situation. When the enemy attempted to flank his position with a vehicle-borne improvised explosive device, Petty Officer Keating led a team to intercept and neutralize the threat with precise sniper and rocket fire," the Navy citation read.

Charlie looked so good that day, I snapped a screenshot of him.

But on this call, he looked different. His face had thinned. One eye was larger than the other, as if he hadn't been sleeping. Black soot, or something like that, peppered his face. He appeared and sounded tired.

I'm his mom and knew the answer before I asked if he was okay. And I knew he wouldn't admit how he felt.

"Yeah, I'm okay," he replied.

"You look exhausted," I told him.

"I haven't been sleeping. I was fighting fires all night."

"Fighting fires? Is that code for something?"

When your son is a Navy SEAL, you become accustomed to not knowing everything.

"No, real fires," Charlie said. "Our camp was burning. We had to put it out."

"Why you? Was ISIS trying to burn you out?"

"No," he said, "we have to."

"I thought you were protecting a dam."

"Well, we are, but we have this other thing going on too."

This other thing?

I knew we were getting into sensitive areas Charlie couldn't talk about. So I started telling him about how well Ali was doing in school. His youngest sister was a little behind in school, and Charlie was the perfect big brother to her. In every photo of Charlie and Ali together, Charlie had an arm around his sister or a hand on her shoulder, making some type of loving contact. Ali adored her big brother. The last time Charlie had come to see us in Florida, three months before this deployment, he had scheduled the trip to be here for Ali's twelfth birthday. We went to Universal Studios, and Charlie and his fiancée, Brooke, wanted to take Ali off by themselves to spend some time with her. When we met up again, Ali beamed, showing off the magic wand Charlie had bought her. Charlie treated Ali like a queen.

Charlie perked up a little as we discussed Ali, but I wasn't sure what else we could talk about and didn't want to keep him awake long.

"I love you," I said. "I'm proud of you."

"I love you," he replied—as always.

"Take care," I told him. "Eat more. Get some sleep."

"Oh, Mom. I'm fine. Don't worry."

I clicked off the call. Remorse came over me for cutting the call short. I went into our bathroom to tell Ron, my husband, about the conversation.

"God, I wish I could have kept Charlie on the phone," I said. "I felt like I needed to talk to him longer."

"Maybe you could have talked to him about the weather," Ron said.

I agreed. Talking about the weather with a SEAL was harmless. Plus, that often proved effective at keeping a conversation going by transitioning into non-sensitive topics.

"I'll talk about the weather next time I talk to him," I said.

Chapter 3

May 2, 2016

Monday morning I woke up nervous and agitated, stomach wrenching. Charlie was on my mind. Especially those fires. Charlie had told me he didn't anticipate much action on this deployment, and instead of serving in a combat role, his team's primary responsibility would be guarding a strategic area. The threat of ISIS fires didn't match those expectations. I hadn't heard from other sources of fires in their area, and the "Rambo" incident hadn't followed that plan, either.

Ron, an orthopedic surgeon, left our Ponte Vedra Beach home at 6:00 a.m. to see patients in Jacksonville, at his office across town. My oldest daughter, Adele, was flying in for a visit that afternoon. Until she arrived, I would be alone on what already was feeling like one of the strangest days of my life.

Running releases my anxiety, so I took Ali to school and headed directly to the beach.

At 8:30, I texted Charlie from the beach: "Really thinking about u right now. I love you. Mom."

I couldn't shake the idea that something was happening with him. It was the middle of the afternoon in Iraq. I called Charlie, and he didn't answer, so I was resigned to the fact that I'd have to wait to hear from him this time.

Typically, I'd run two or three miles down the beach. But this day, I couldn't even run a mile. On the verge of an anxiety attack, I turned and started going back to my car. I prayed. I started to say a Rosary. I couldn't shake my uneasy feelings. While walking, I looked out over the ocean and into the patchwork of clouds.

"Charlie," I said softly, "I hope you're okay."

Then I felt something being yanked directly from my heart. I couldn't grab it and bring it back. It was such a strong pull that I put my hand to my chest.

What if he isn't okay? Has he been killed?

We'd have to fly to California, to where he was stationed in Coronado. I had a fear of flying. How could I fly all the way across the country, knowing my son was dead? I hadn't handled funerals well—I stopped attending them. How could I handle a funeral for Charlie?

In a matter of seconds, my mind covered the thirty-one years of Charlie's life. He was my oldest of four children, so I spent the most time bringing him up, protecting him. I remembered when he was first born, how big his mouth seemed—until he gave me his huge smile. I gazed in awe at him snuggled next to me in the hospital and wondered what great things he was going to do in his life. I then pictured all the training I coached him through as a successful runner. I couldn't bear the thought of living my life without Charlie. He was the leader of our family, a mentor to his brother and a guardian to his two sisters. His smile, his funny, goofy stories, his sibling wars, and his all-American patriotism.

It's so conflicting, wanting your son to become a Navy SEAL. On one hand, you are praying that they succeed to the Olympic status of the military, and, on the other hand, you are praying that they don't die in battle. It is well known that being a SEAL is the ultimate test of manhood.

I remembered when Charlie entered INDOC (Indoctrination), the holding tank for students waiting to start BUD/S, or the Basic Underwater Demolition/SEAL. All Navy SEALs must graduate from a twenty-four-week school as their first step to being a SEAL. That is BUD/S. Then, a basic parachutist course and a twenty-six-week SEAL Qualification Training called SQT.

There was a website for the mothers of BUD/S Class 266. This was Charlie's class. After verifying my connection to Charlie, I was accepted into the group. We could talk to each other on-line about our sons' progress and what we knew. Joining other mothers who had children with the drive to become a SEAL was comforting. Even though I wasn't able to see their faces, I was grateful for the community. Still, it was a stressful experience.

Every morning I woke up to comments such as, "I'm out," or "Bye, ladies," or "My son didn't make it. Nice to know you."

I began to dread going to the online group because it made me worry that it might happen to Charlie. The further he progressed in the program, the more of these comments I saw each morning. We had started on the website with close to 400 moms, but almost a year later, as our sons' training came to an end, only seventeen were left. I felt fortunate to be one of them.

At the SEALs' graduation, we were already friends. It felt like a reunion of sorts, finally meeting each other in person. We also compared notes as to what each of our boys told us about the other. It was a fun game that strengthened our community of mothers.

Somehow, deep in my heart, I knew Charlie would make it. Still, I did worry.

I wanted very much for him to make the SEAL Team, but in the back of my mind it wasn't winning a race and earning a medal—it was protecting and fighting for our country and that could be fatal.

While keeping up my pace on the beach, I was so deep in thought that I didn't even pick up a perfect shark tooth in the sand. Gazing out to the ocean again, I recalled Charlie's first challenge, when he was only two-and-a-half years old. We were in London on business.

The concierge at the Savoy had arranged for a wonderful older lady to babysit in our room so we could go to dinner. Charlie's dad and I thought it would be nice to have some time together without the kids.

It was difficult to even obtain reservations at this upscale restaurant and usually you had to make those reservations weeks in advance. We arrived a little early and went to the bar to have a drink while waiting for our table.

Then, just as the maître d' called us, a woman came running up and asked if we were the Keatings. She said, "They said they have a problem at the hotel, and you need to go back now!"

We hurried back to find that Charlie, an active little boy, had been jumping on the bed and hit one of the pictures on the wall. The picture fell and the glass broke, cutting Charlie badly between his eyes. He did not like the sight of his own blood and was screaming.

After finding a doctor through the hotel, we made it to a hospital where they strapped Charlie into a constricting cradleboard, like a papoose, and sent him into the operating room. Parents were not allowed to accompany their child. We could hear him screaming, though. I felt so nauseated. They put the stitches in with no anesthetic. Charlie made a full recovery, but retained a lifetime signature scar like Harry Potter's—which, of course, any boy would love. I hated to see him already with a scar on his face, but the more he grew the less you could see it.

As a young boy, he knew how to have fun—like jumping on the bed at the hotel. While we were in Switzerland, we were near a pool in a tourist area in Lausanne. Charlie, two-and-a-half years old, jumped into the pool. Some Germans nearby panicked, seeing such a young boy in the pool, and two of them were about to jump in to save him.

Before they could, I yelled, "No! No! It's okay! He can swim!"

Of course, they probably didn't understand English and likely thought I was afraid he was going to drown.

Charlie turned around in the water, smiled at them, and started laughing as he swam to the side of the pool. Understandably, they were amazed and a bit embarrassed. But then, there aren't many swimming pools in Germany, compared to the many pools and canals in Phoenix, Arizona.

While still walking on the beach, I heard Charlie's unmistakable voice in my head interrupting the memories.

"Mom, you can do it," I heard him tell me. *"You're going to have to do it. You're strong. You're going to have to do it for me."*

Charlie's words, as so often had been the case, calmed me. A sense of relief came over me. My thinking shifted.

You know how you imagine things might happen, but they never do, I reminded myself. *Besides, you never felt like this when he was deployed before. He's well-trained, and he has always come back okay.*

At my car, I noticed the time. I'd have to rush to the airport for Adele's arrival. The entire way to the airport, a seesaw of emotions grappled with me. I knew something was happening with Charlie. Next, I'd tell myself it was foolish to think so negatively. I'd hear from him soon and everything would be fine—like it always was with Charlie, even from his youngest days when he showed a deft touch at slipping out of trouble's grasp.

At the airport, I asked Adele to drive. "I'm out of sorts," I said. "I don't feel well."

On the way home, I told Adele everything from the past two days. I didn't feel any better after Ali came home from school and started her homework.

As the night wound down, I felt too anxious to sleep. I took an Ambien and went to bed early. Not even a sleeping pill could help me sleep.

Chapter 4

May 3, 2016

At 5:00 a.m. Tuesday, I gave up on sleeping. Military parents learn which internet sites provide news from where their children are serving. I started searching for news from Iraq on my iPad. I turned on the TV and heard Fox News report that a US soldier had been killed near the dam in Teleskof, in northern Iraq. Charlie was in Teleskof.

I knew right then—Charlie was the one killed. I prayed he wasn't … but I knew.

I texted Charlie to check on him. No answer. My anxiety heightened. I kept monitoring TV news and the Internet. Fox News continued to report the death of a US serviceman, but provided no details.

I made breakfast for Ron and he went to the office. I texted as many people I knew that might have heard from Charlie. I focused on getting Ali ready for school.

I called Ron at his office. "It was Charlie," I told him. "It had to be Charlie. I can feel it."

Ron tried to sound reassuring, but I could detect worry in his voice as he replied, "No, it's not. Don't worry, it's not Charlie." He was starting to see patients.

My mother called. She'd heard the same media reports. "That's near where Charlie is."

I said, "I really think it's Charlie."

My sister in Ohio texted: "Is Charlie all right?"

I called her. "Strange that you ask, because I feel like it might be him," I told her. "I'm waiting to hear something from anyone."

I continued to text other friends of Charlie.

My phone started blowing up with texts from concerned family members and friends. I felt like I'd waited for hours without hearing or reading anything new since the original report.

At 8:13 a.m., I sent Charlie another text: "U and team OK?"

Again, no reply.

We have thousands of military members over there, I told myself. *There's no way that's Charlie.*

But I knew it was. He was his Team's leader. If anyone was going to take a bullet for the rest of the Team, it would be Charlie. He'd give his life to prevent anything from happening to one of his brothers.

I needed to get out of the house. I'd planned on playing tennis that morning at the courts a half-mile from our home.

I remembered playing tennis with Charlie when he visited with my all-girls tennis league. The coach asked us to pick a partner to play against each other. I looked at Charlie and, grinning, he looked at me.

One of the ladies yelled, "I'll take the SEAL!"

It was decided. The woman loved it, Charlie being the only guy to venture out and play against his mom!

At the tennis court on May 3, one of my friends said, "You seem nervous."

"I'm fine," I replied. "I just need to play tennis."

Tennis would be my distraction. We hadn't been playing long, and I actually was playing better than usual, when my phone rang in the middle of one of my serves. I stopped.

"I'm sorry," I told my playing partners. "I hate to do this, but I need to answer my phone."

The only thing I heard on the other end of the phone was: "It was him."

I screamed and dropped my racket. A loud, guttural scream.

I immediately started running toward our home, phone still to my ear and tears cascading down my cheeks.

The next thing I remember is dashing into Adele's room and waking her up. "Adele! Something really bad has just happened!"

"Is it Ron?" she screamed, knowing it was bad. "What happened to Ron?"

"No! It's Charlie! He was killed in Iraq!"

Adele started screaming and crying. I had to make myself stop my crying to comfort her. We sat on her bed, holding each other tightly.

One of my friends from the tennis court, Marnie, had followed me home. She came into Adele's room. "What can I do?" she asked.

I was still trying to console Adele. "Charlie's in heaven," I told Adele. "He's with all our dogs, your grandparents." I turned to Marnie. "Can you call the priest?"

I called Ron.

"Oh my God," I said between sobs, "it was Charlie."

"No! No!" Ron yelled. "I'm coming home."

Ron was an hour away, but I desperately wanted him home when official notification of Charlie's death came.

Our neighborhood had a guard gate for admitting guests. On Charlie's last visit we had walked the beach, and I joked that if he ever was killed in action, I would instruct the guards not to allow the Navy's notification officers past the gate.

"So, nothing can happen to you," I told him, drawing a laugh.

Now, here I was in that very position, where the notification team would be entering through that gate and driving up to our house.

Fortunately, Ron made it home before the notification came. He burst through the door in tears, and he, Adele, and I hugged each other, sobbing.

Charlie was only five years old when I met Ron and nine when we married. Even though Ron was Charlie's stepfather, and Ron had a son, Jeremy, from a previous marriage, Ron and

Charlie were as close as any biological father and son. Ron, a former Olympic athlete, was actively involved in Charlie's sports and taught him to ski and paraglide and a long list of other adventurous activities. Ron and Charlie were buddies, and so special was their relationship that Ron may have been the most emotional about the news.

With Ron home, I kept watching out the front door for an unmarked car to pull up to our curb. Even as what would have been lunchtime—our stomachs were too nauseated to eat—came and went, we had received no notification.

I wondered why, as the next of kin, I hadn't already been notified.

Maybe it actually wasn't Charlie who was killed, I hoped. *There's a lot of military personnel there. They could have made a mistake.*

But I couldn't convince myself. I was hoping against facts.

Finally, around 2:00 p.m., through the same glass front door that I had watched Charlie's taillights pull away barely four months earlier, I saw a small, nondescript, tan sedan pull up, containing four people wearing US Navy uniforms. The car seemed uncomfortably small for four adults.

As they exited the car and started up the sidewalk, I forced myself to stop crying and turned to go sit on the couch. Adele sat to my left and placed her right arm around my shoulders, tissues for the two of us in her other hand.

The doorbell rang, and Ron opened the door for the notification team and then came around the couch to stand behind me. One female chaplain and three men took positions standing in front of us. The men looked nervous, inexperienced even. I felt sorry for them that they had to deliver this news.

One of the officers handed me a piece of paper and started talking as though he was reciting from a handbook. "It is my duty to inform you that Charles Keating the Fourth, a Navy SEAL, was killed in Iraq today, May 3, 2016."

"What time was he killed?" I blurted out. I'd had that horrible feeling the morning before.

The officers' facial expressions indicated my question had derailed them from their script.

"Nine thirty," the man said.

I was looking down at the paper as he answered. The sheet said Charlie had been killed on May 2.

"What date did you say?" I asked.

"May 3."

The notification sheet had a typo.

The officer paused as if to gather his thoughts, and then started to share the circumstances of Charlie's death.

Ron asked, "Why did it take you so long to get here?"

"His next of kin had to be informed first," the man replied.

"She is his next of kin," Ron said, pointing to me. "She's his mother."

"No," the man said, "his wife is the next of kin. We had to notify his wife first."

His wife? I smiled.

The officer, in a tone surprisingly rude for the circumstances, asked me, "Why are you smiling?"

"I didn't know he got married," I said. "I thought he was going to get married in November. But I'd told him he should get married secretly."

"It seems as though he did," the officer said, "and it seems you already knew we were coming to notify you of his death."

My thought was: *That's not very nice to say to someone who just lost their son.*

But my response was: "I just knew it was my son when I first heard someone had been killed in that area. Plus, there are ways to find out things in the (military) community."

The officer stopped his questioning and concluded by informing us of the arrangements being made to ship Charlie's body back to the US and of the official services.

* * *

The last time Charlie and I walked on the beach, we discussed what would happen if he died in combat. Because of his name, I told him, the press would be all over the story. Charlie had grown up having to answer that, yes, his name came from *that* Charles Keating. And despite his grandfather's involvement in one of our country's most infamous savings and loan scandals, Charlie always embraced his name and family roots.

Sure enough, the name *Charles Humphrey Keating IV* immediately drew attention. I had wanted him to have his own name or, if that wouldn't work, change the *H* name to my maiden name, Holmes, so he would not have to be the fourth. I never thought a child should be responsible for their elders' mistakes.

Shortly after the four Navy officers left our home, someone posted "RIP Charlie" on Facebook. The news quickly spread.

By the time we were told, reports—like the one on Facebook—were already starting to spread.

Florida Governor Rick Scott called to offer his condolences. He had appointed me to a hospital board I served on, and I knew that Governor Scott had served in the Navy and his father in the Army. The pain came through his voice as he greeted me.

"This is just so tough for our Navy and for our country," he told me. "Your son's sacrifice won't be forgotten."

I needed to hear that last part. The governor informed me that flags in Florida would be flown at half-mast in honor of Charlie and another SEAL who had died in training a few weeks earlier. The governor gave me his cell phone number and told me to call if our family needed anything.

Ron DeSantis, our US Representative in Washington, DC, now the governor of Florida, called wanting to name a post office in my hometown for Charlie. Indiana Governor Mike Pence, now the vice president of the United States, informed me that the flags would be lowered for my son because Charlie had attended college in Indiana, at IU.

Soon, reporters came to the gate of our neighborhood seeking interviews, but they weren't allowed in. I had a string of voicemails from reporters from all over the country and Canada and Australia, but I didn't return any of their calls. After a while, we decided to consent to one interview. We were receiving word of reports that I lived in Coronado and Arizona, and we wanted the reports to be accurate and to ensure that Charlie's story would be appropriately remembered as more of the world learned of his death. We met a Fox regional television reporter in front of our house and did a short interview, and let that interview get picked up nationally.

With the widespread publicity surrounding Charlie's sacrifice, I knew we had to tell Ali and I anticipated it would be difficult. We asked friends to pick her up from school and take her to their house. She'd already experienced that break from her daily routine, and before she came home, we decided to keep things as normal as possible for her by having dinner and helping her with her schoolwork before we told her about Charlie.

We put on our brave faces when Ali arrived.

But when she walked in, she glanced around and asked me, "What's wrong?"

"Well," I said, "we have something to tell you, and it's about Charlie."

I paused to allow her to process that I had news about her brother.

"Charlie died in combat," I said, "and he's in heaven."

"Oh no," she said.

I couldn't hold back my tears any longer.

"Why are you crying?" she asked.

"We're going to miss him," I told her.

"He's in heaven, Mommy," she said. "You shouldn't be crying."

Oh, my sweet Ali! Her words were beautiful but heart-ripping.

Chapter 5

The Day My Music Died

As reported by news media CNN, *Military Times*, *The New York Times*, and *The Washington Post*, Charlie's death went like this:

Charlie Keating IV and his SEAL Team, as a quick reaction force, were supporting Peshmerga forces near the Iraqi town of Teleskof, a Christian community located approximately eighteen miles north of Mosul. ISIS had covertly formed an attack force of 125 fighters and 20 vehicles, which included several truck bombs, some bulldozers, and their infantry. They assaulted the Kurdish Peshmerga and attempted to capture Teleskof, located about three miles in front of their position. Initially, the ISIS forces attacked through the forward lines of defense and over-whelmed the Peshmerga as they moved toward Teleskof.

ISIS led the attack at about 7:30 a.m., local time, with the suicide truck bombers breaching the Peshmerga lines and de-stroying an Iraqi checkpoint. Three suicide truck bombers were followed by bulldozers that cleared the road of the wreckage of the exploding trucks. The remaining ISIS vehicles and troops then attempted to go into the town to secure it.

There was a twelve-man US Army adviser team with the Peshmerga under attack, and about twenty minutes after the ISIS attack began, this team reported that it was in contact with the enemy and needed assistance. US forces had preassembled the quick reaction force (QRF), of which Charlie was a member, to assist these forces in such a situation, and Charlie and his twenty-man QRF team rushed to the scene to try to evacuate the adviser team and assist the Peshmerga.

Coalition spokesman Army Col. Steve Warren later said, "The mission for Keating's quick reaction force was to focus on extracting the American service members caught in the fight. ... The enemy was able to very covertly assemble enough force, which included the several truck bombs, some bulldozers, and of course their infantry. And they were available to punch through the Kurdish line there, punch through the [forward line of troops] and really sprint towards Teleskof, which was their objective."

The Baghdad-based spokesman for the US Defense Department told reporter Andrew Tilghman with *Navy Times*, "There were bullets everywhere."

As the battle progressed, the SEALs ran low on ammunition, and then Charlie's machine gun malfunctioned, so he ran back to a nearby coalition vehicle for more ammunition and a new weapon.

Armed with a sniper rifle, Charlie climbed to the roof of a building and began firing at the ISIS fighters. The fighting continued for two more hours before Charlie was struck by small arms fire from the enemy at about 9:32 a.m. He continued returning fire on the enemy until he passed out. Despite receiving small arms fire from ISIS, two medevac helicopters were called, and evacuated Charlie within an hour of being hit. His wound, however, was not survivable and Charlie died. His flight became what is known as a "Hero Flight"—carrying the body of a soldier killed in combat. Both medevac helicopters were hit by ISIS fire from the ground, but were not disabled.

The US responded to the ISIS attack with fighters, bombers, and drones carrying out thirty-one airstrikes, which killed fifty-eight ISIS militants and destroyed twenty enemy vehicles, thus saving the village and the trapped US advisors.

I, however, learned later, so much more when I attended his funeral. I spoke to commanders, other Team 1 members that were

with him, the medic, and his friends. I learned that he was re-
ferred to as "Chuck" by all. This came about because when they
were on the radio, the word "Charlie" was used as a platoon call
sign. To this day, I know who served with Charlie; when they talk
to me, they refer to him as Chuck.

The other thing I learned by Charlie's death was that I am
now a Gold Star Mother and we are a Gold Star Family. I had
never heard of this before, and now I hear about this too much.
Now I notice when someone else is a Gold Star Family and it
makes me feel sad. It is not something you want to be, yet it is a
way to distinguish our family for my son's sacrifice.

I found that after all pertinent information is dispersed to the
families, it seems the Gold Star Families put things together in
detail and look at how it happened that their family member was
killed. We all wonder what our loved one was feeling and if he
suffered.

I have my own thoughts, based on the input I have heard and
read, and feel I can now visualize how Charlie/Chuck was killed.

> On the morning of May 3, Charlie had just
> heard that the American advisors in the village
> were being overrun by a surprise ISIS attack.
>
> Charlie, being the leader of his platoon, said,
> "We're going!" He ran to the fight.
>
> They jumped into their unarmored vehicles.
> As they moved into the area, the vehicles were
> hit with a rocket-propelled grenade. The SEAL
> Team took cover after scrambling from the dam-
> aged trucks. Watching the "Vice News" video on
> the Internet, which features original videos from
> around the world, I could follow the action. The
> SEALs were behind the wreckage of the explod-
> ed trucks. They were firing machine guns. That's
> when Charlie's gun jammed and, in the video, I
> saw him running to the back of an open truck and

grab what looked like a sniper rifle. Then he ran to the left, through gunfire, toward a large, many-storied red building.

That building is where a sniper would go to get the "high ground" in a firefight. Charlie and another sniper made it to the top of the roof and went up against a wall and watched bullets fly over their heads.

Charlie reached down into his pants pocket and pulled out Chapstick. He grinned at his partner and put it on. Sliding his hand down the side of his leg, returning the Chapstick, he smiled and said, "Let's go."

At that point, they proceeded to engage the enemy. During the long firefight, the communication equipment was spotty and was being jammed by ISIS. Chuck and the other SEALs entered the fight and communicated by yelling or hand signals.

Their positions suddenly came under intense enemy-flanking fire, and Chuck noticed one of the ISIS snipers was getting a "good read" on the Team, and knew that an accurate enemy sniper could wreak havoc on his Team. Chuck backed up a little to try to get a "bead on him." As he maneuvered, he was hit by a bullet that squeezed through the small seam between the two plates of his bulletproof vest. Chuck reported being hit, but said he was okay and kept shooting.

"Damn, my arm is hit. I'm good," he said as he kept trying to maneuver.

Bullets were flying everywhere. He turned his head camera off. This was an unusual thing.

As his mom, I have my thoughts as to why he turned off his head camera. A few weeks before he was killed, I sent Charlie a video of an incompetent ISIS militant fumbling around with grenades and shooting at the Iraqi soldiers. The man recording the video had a head camera on. We watched from his perspective of how unprofessional these untrained ISIS guys were. Then the man taking the video was hit, and you saw that the head cam fell to the ground and stopped. It was chilling.

I feel that Charlie knew he was in a dangerous situation and didn't want his mom to see a similar video.

Eventually, he collapsed with a smile on his face. He died quickly since he was hit in the heart by a bullet through the small seam under his arm, between his armored plates.

Many men around him tried their best to save him. Team members did extraordinary things to try to save him. One SEAL was also wounded when he ran out under fire and dragged Chuck to cover. Another man rammed a truck through a heavy barrier, with gates flying, to transport him to the helicopter. A medic did everything and more than he had to, to try to save him. I am grateful for these men's efforts and know they were doing everything they could to save my son.

A fellow SEAL officer-friend wrote in a letter: "Personally, I enviously followed Charlie's accolades whether he was deployed or back in San Diego. I would read numerous reports, searching for 'Keating,' to keep tabs on whatever operation or training event he was involved with. At this point I imagine you have heard about his repeated acts of heroism and this note will likely only serve to reiterate your son's brave actions under such extreme circumstances. On the day that we lost him, he was doing what we hope each one of us would have the courage to do in a similar situation, aggressively and without hesitation attacking a ruthless enemy to protect his teammates. I learned how he selflessly maneuvered to provide effective fire against a formidable force that was attacking his teammates and our allies. The fact that he was putting himself in harm's way for his teammates likely never crossed his mind; a true mark of a SEAL warrior."

I believe Charlie/Chuck died with a smile on his face because he knew he had finished his mission on earth and he was lucky to have his time. I feel that Jesus came to greet my son and take him to a better place.

PART II

Raising a Navy SEAL

Chapter 6

Savings and Loan Scandal of the 1980s

"Mommy! Somebody is at the door!"

"No, Charlie, don't open the door. It might be a stranger," I said as I shifted the baby on my hip. "I'll get it."

When I opened the door, a man and a woman, strangers, both wearing suits and looking official, were standing there.

Oddly, they didn't say anything but were glancing around behind me while I was absorbed with keeping Charlie from going outside. I thought they might be church missionaries.

I said, "Charlie, stop pushing the door. You're not going out."

Then, a bit impatient, I turned to the couple and said, "Yes. What is it you want?"

The man said, "We need to talk to you."

I said, "Well, who are you?"

The man said, "You're Mrs. Keating," in an impatient voice. "Do you live in this house alone, Mrs. Keating?"

Before I could answer, the woman said, "How's the baby? Oh, is this Adele? Is she feeling better?"

Adele had been in intensive care due to a virus when she was born.

I replied that she was fine, and the woman asked, "How are you feeling after your cancer surgery?"

I wondered how they would know about my surgery. The doctor had discovered a tumor on my thyroid after Adele was born. It was cancer, and I had to stop nursing Adele so I could have my thyroid removed.

The woman said, "Your daughter looks wonderful. It's so difficult to have a sick baby, isn't it?"

The man said, "Did your husband help you buy this home?"

I demanded, "Who are you?"

She said, apologetically, "We are from the FBI."

They showed me their badges.

He said, harshly, "Hey, we have to come in!"

I had read books and seen TV shows about the good cop, bad cop approach, but I didn't realize they actually did that and was surprised it was happening to me. Here I was, twenty-eight years old, with three little kids, fighting cancer, getting divorced, in multiple lawsuits—and now the FBI was at my door. At that moment I realized my phone was tapped and we were being followed wherever we went. Sounds strange, but that turned out to be a reality.

The man took a step toward me and said sternly, "We'd like to talk to you about your husband."

My stomach tightened. Would they think I was implicated in the Keating savings and loan situation? I tried to send Charlie down the hall; I didn't want him to hear anything bad about his father. Charlie was four, and he had "big ears" and liked to know about everything going on, so keeping him insulated was not easy. I could tell he was afraid and was not going far.

There was no way I could tell if the badges were authentic and I was too embarrassed to inspect them, although I thought to myself, *I'm a Keating. Oh my God, the FBI is at my door!*

I relaxed a bit when the woman gently asked, "Is your husband helping you at all? May we come in and talk? Confidentially, of course."

The man, in an impatient tone, stated, "Yes, we need to come in and talk to you."

I asked them if they had a search warrant, and they said they did not. In a way, I wanted to say, "Come on in and sit down."

The woman seemed kind, but something about her conversation just didn't ring true.

They knew everything about me.

Because of the situation with the savings and loan disaster and the divorce, I was inundated with paperwork. I had files for the IRS, FBI, FDIC, and RICO lawsuits on my dining room table. I had a bankruptcy attorney. I had a federal attorney. I had a divorce attorney.

I didn't want them to see what I had and go through my papers. I also had the kids there and would not be able to control them and deal with these strangers at the same time.

I said, "I have an attorney here in Phoenix. You can contact him," and gave them his name.

Then I gathered up my courage and said, "If you want to talk to me, I need to be subpoenaed."

After the FBI couple had left, I frantically called my attorney, saying, "The FBI came to my door! What should I do?"

There was no possibility of criminal activity in my job in marketing. I was not involved in decisions involving company policy or company funds.

Still, I was concerned. What if there was something they thought I was involved in? Could I be in trouble for having Keating as my last name? What would happen to the children if, somehow, I was sent to prison? Charlie IV was four years old and little Adele was barely one year old.

My attorney reemphasized previous advice. "Krista, you must get out of any involvement with the Keatings as soon as humanly possible. If both parents are in jail, there is no future for your kids."

That was the deciding factor, as well as the terrified look on Charlie's face. The other children did not even understand what was going on, but my oldest son did. He already knew his father and I were not living in the same house, and the three of them visited their father every other weekend, and then eventually spending part of their summer with him in Coronado, California.

Chapter 7

A Name

Charles Humphrey Keating, Charles Humphrey Keating Jr., Charles Humphrey Keating III, Charles Humphrey Keating IV. … The past deeds of the grandfathers and fathers with the same name is a lot of weight on a young boy's life. When Charlie was born, his name meant "greatness and success"; when he was two years old, his name meant "scandal." Most every child loves his name. So little Charlie did not necessarily understand why everyone knew his name and the reaction could be different.

Going to the grocery store was always a challenge. I would have Adele in the baby seat and Charlie was supposed to hold on to the side of the cart, staying with us. He was not supposed to let go. There was not much room for groceries, but that's how it was, being a single mother. As most parents know, the grocery store is the best place for children to cause and get into trouble.

After finishing my shopping and heading to the checkout, I noticed that Mr. Keating Jr.'s face was on three different magazines. Of course, to the kids, that was "Papa." An older couple in front of us at the checkout commented on the cover of one of the magazines. The husband told his wife to "look at that crook, Charlie Keating." He continued to say how he couldn't believe what he did.

His wife replied, "Be quiet, you never know who is around here, and he's from here."

Charlie, not shy, heard his name. "I'm Charlie Keating!" he

boasted.

I said to the couple, "Uh, yes, he's Charlie Keating and that's his grandfather."

Mortified, the woman not only hit her husband with her purse, but yelled in his ear all the way out the door.

On another occasion, Charlie was supposed to continue holding on to the side of the shopping cart, but as we were checking out he spotted the gumball machine. As I finished paying, I looked up to see Charlie standing there with his hand halfway up the machine, trying to reach for a gumball.

"What are you doing? Stop, Charlie, we don't have money for that today," I said.

"Mom, I'm stuck and can't get my hand out," he yelled.

I tried to pull it out. Adele was scared that he would be there forever.

I tried and tried, but couldn't remove it. When the manager arrived, he was not happy. He asked our names. Telling him seemed to make him more unhappy. He thought we would sue the store. He called the fire department.

Once the fire department got there, Charlie thought this was really cool. I was not pleased. They were able to free his hand, and the manager breathed a sigh of relief. He brought Charlie a Pepsi, which upset me because he was rewarding Charlie for his behavior. I, instead, had a talk with him about stealing. Back home, we baked cookies, and we delivered them to the fire department, apologizing for wasting their time.

In 1995, Charlie, then ten years old, was running a mile in under five-and-a-half minutes, and he qualified for his first US Track and Field Nationals in the "ten and under" category. The whole family flew to Sacramento, California.

Charlie qualified for the finals, and as the runners were lining up, preparing to start the race, an announcer read off the names.

When he read Charlie's name, he said, "Oh! Charles Keating. What a loser."

With tearful eyes, Charlie looked up at me.

I was at the fence, where Charlie could hear me. I thought, *Are you kidding!* I said, "Charlie, don't listen to him. You just run faster! Prove to them you are who you are."

He ran a good race and finished in the top ten of about sixty racers. After the race, I confronted the referee, who apologized profusely. I think he thought the name was a coincidence. That out-of-place comment may have inspired Charlie to run better, but it troubled him for a long time.

Charlie learned to deal with this after a problem at school. An older boy told Charlie his face looked like it had been smashed in an elevator. When Charlie informed me about the incident, I told him he needed to be able to laugh at himself, and if it happened again, he should scrunch up his face in front of the boy and laugh. He did that, and it worked. Both boys laughed, and the teasing stopped. So whenever there was an incident with his name, he learned to make a joke and laugh it off. In his heart, he still loved his name and his grandfather.

After the meet, the kids and I were on the plane, going home. With only three seats in each row, Charlie, as the oldest child, was up front, seated next to a gentleman, apart from the rest of us. Charlie, even as a youngster, was personable and made friends easily, even with adults. He talked with people, smiled constantly, and had the special sparkle that few people—whether children or adults—are blessed with.

During the flight, I kept an eye on him. He was happily engaged in conversation with the man seated next to him. I figured Charlie was telling him about his experience running in the Nationals. He never looked back at us and was completely engrossed in his conversation. And I could see he was doing more than his share of the talking.

After we landed and got off the plane, the man who had been seated with Charlie came up to us, shook my hand, introduced himself, and said, "My God! You're wonderful. What a family! What a life! You have the best life. I cannot believe it. Your son told me this story about you guys and his dad and the savings and loan scandal."

I thought, *Really? Charlie!*

Later, we had a little talk about how much we tell people about our private lives. At the same time, I realized this was Charlie's personality.

Living with someone else's name can be a hindrance and a gift. After a certain amount of time, people forget what the scandal was and only remember the name. This can help you open a door for an interview or a conversation. Eventually, people might think you're that famous actor, Charles Keating, from the soap opera world.

Over the years and on another occasion, when Charlie was back in Scottsdale, he met Mike Tyson, the famous boxer. Mike Tyson thought the world of Charlie's grandfather, even though he was in prison at the time. Tyson was impressed with Charles Jr. because he had stood up against the government.

"Hey! You're Charlie Keating. He's my buddy!" Mike said, and put Charlie IV in a headlock.

Since both of them lived in the area, they often ran into each other and, each time, Tyson put Charlie in a headlock and "threw" him around a little. Charlie had a good sense of humor and enjoyed their brief friendship when they happened to meet.

Charlie, 15 months old, swimming.

"Harry Potter" scar in London.

Learning to sail in Mexico with Granpa Bill Holmes.

Learning to surf in Mexico with Grandpa Bill.

Our family motto. Attitude is Everything!

Charlie, third from the left, at the start of
1995 National USTA track finals.

Tickle time!

Charlie at 12, and Krista at 12,
Scottsdale, Arizona. Charlie broke
a 5-minute mile.

Ron and his sister, Vivian, Olympic Bronze
medal Pairs Figure Skating team.

Start of a blended family:
Jeremy, 12; Charlie 5, and Adele, 2.

Charlie skiing.

Visiting Mexico and getting to know each other.

Charlie starting high school.

Stepdad fun, skiing with Ron.

Charlie learning to paraglide in Aspen, Colorado.

As a young man, Charlie frequently
wore a Navy SEAL shirt.

Steeplechase champion.

Krista coaching her son, Charlie, after a race.

Charlie winning a
cross country meet.

Charlie loved to dress up not only
as "Rambo" but as a "cool" teammate for Arcadia High School.

Charlie and his mom at his graduation
from Arcadia High School.

Chapter 8

Running from Divorce

With my work, advertising and marketing for restaurants, and taking care of three small children, I had stopped running. Running had always been a part of my life. Now, with the divorce pending, the FBI looming in the background, and a tight financial situation, I felt the need to clear my head, so I started running again.

The cool thing about my grade school in Scottsdale, Arizona, in the 1960s, had been a requirement from the physical education department, starting in the second grade, that all students had to work up to run a mile every day before they participated in PE. Most of the students walked or jogged the four laps, including me, to be with friends.

At some point in the year, Ms. Kelson, our PE teacher at Navajo Elementary, organized races. She put me in the 100-yard dash, where a big girl, who was very fast, had beat me every time. One day, Ms. Kelson decided to organize a long run going around the field, then the park, and around a second field. She had invited the parents to come and watch. Everyone was excited.

I was quite small, and thought, *Oh, this big girl is going to beat me again. This giant girl. I'm so sick of being creamed.*

We started with everyone running in a pack. We ran around the first field, and over a hill in the park, where the parents lost sight of us. As we ran farther and farther, one by one, the girls dropped out and walked. I kept on running and pretty soon I was by myself.

My parents said they were sitting there waiting when they suddenly saw a little girl, way out front, coming up the hill, waving at them.

They said, "Is that Krista? Krista! Oh my God!"

I had not only beaten the big girl, but I had also won the race. In the ensuing years, I kept on winning. Eventually, I won the high school girls' state mile and subsequently earned a running scholarship to the University of Arizona.

Now looking back, I believe I was lucky to find my talent. Running continued to make me feel better and also gave me a goal.

Charlie watched me run every day. Then I started racing in local 5Ks, where sometimes he would ride his bike next to me. My parents had my other kids on the sidelines, cheering for me. One day, Charlie said he wanted to run a 5K with me. I was concerned because it was three miles—a long way for a five-year-old. Telling Charlie he couldn't do something definitely only made him persist more, so I finally agreed to let him run with me.

At the start of the race, I told him, "Whenever you need to slow down, let me know, and we'll walk."

He didn't say anything and kept on running, smiling all the way. When we finished, he was in first place in the "six and under" age group. He wasn't even tired and was looking forward to the next time he could run in a race.

The greatest thing about that day was he *won*! Charlie never forgot how it felt to be first.

The small gesture of my running for mental health conformed our entire family into a running family. Charlie and Adele became National-caliber runners. After getting that part of my life more settled through running, I focused on supporting my children.

I used my marketing degree and was able to find work helping restaurants develop their menus. I arranged promotions for a Mexican restaurant and made $1,000 here and $1,000 there to keep some money coming in. Although money was tight, I was able to scrape by.

One day, I was at a restaurant with some friends. As I was leaving, a man named Ron Joseph came up to me and tried to start a conversation. Still reeling from the effects of going through a divorce, I flatly told him I wasn't interested and I had too much on my plate.

Going through a divorce and thinking of your children while knowing they will never have their same parents together in their home makes you pause. You love your children so much and want to give them everything in life. You want them to be happy. You want to have a *family*.

After the divorce was final, I thought I wouldn't meet anyone who'd want to date me since I had three children. Also, I was religious and went to church with my kids every Sunday. I felt if you can't thank God for an hour a week, you must be pretty selfish. Not many men would fit this bill. He'd have to be his own person, athletic, supportive, funny, and willing to be a stepparent to three children.

Chapter 9

Future Family

Ron Joseph's parents lived in Stuttgart, Germany, where his father was a shoe salesman. Both of his parents were athletes: his mother ran hurdles and his father was a professional soccer player when the Jewish people were still allowed to participate in sports in Germany.

After Adolf Hitler came to power, they were required to wear yellow armbands to be easily identified as Jewish. One of Ron's father's customers was German General Erwin Rommel, who befriended Ron's father and soon advised him to take his wife and leave the country. They came to the United States in 1937.

Ron's mother felt that the family had to assimilate in America, or the Nazis might seek them out and kill them. They learned to speak English and used it rather than their native language. They found jobs and became true American citizens.

Ron was born and raised in Highland Park, Illinois. During his school years in the cold winters of northern Illinois, the school would freeze the back of the schoolyard in the winter so kids could ice skate or play hockey. As a youngster, Ron wasn't a very good skater and wanted to play hockey. He also wanted to be able to beat another kid who always won skating races. Ron decided to take skating lessons.

Ron's mother felt that since she had to drive Ron to skating lessons, she might as well bring his younger sister along to learn to skate. This led to Ron and his sister Vivian learning to figure skate as a pairs team. After hard work and many difficulties, they made it to the Olympic team.

Ron and his sister skated in three world championships and the 1964 Olympics, where they were bronze medalists. They were North American Champions and World Silver Medalists in 1965.

At the end of their competition, Ron decided to go to medical school at Northwestern and then the Mayo Clinic in Rochester, Minnesota. After living through cold winters in Illinois and even colder winters in Minnesota to do his residency, with an adventurous spirit, Ron decided to move to Phoenix, Arizona, an exciting opportunity to see some of the great "Wild West."

My meeting Ron for the first time was by accident. I wasn't ready for dating and told him I had three kids and was trying to make a life for them while dealing with a divorce. My parents lived across the street, and we were all trying to maneuver into a stable routine. So basically, I wasn't interested—but it ended up that the kids were.

When my kids and I returned from a trip to Mexico, where my parents have a cabin, we found three chairs by our back door. One was stacked with stuffed animals and toys for a girl. The other two were overflowing with kites, toy guns, games, and boys' clothing. Ron and his son, twelve-year-old Jeremy, had gone out to make friends with the kids on their own terms!

That was nice, so I told him, "Okay, I'm not interested, but we can be friends if you want. Why don't we go ice skating, since you're an ice skater?"

We did. The kids were enthralled, watching him go out and, first, do a jump and then a double jump on the ice. The two boys were soon skating, with Ron showing them how to skate and slide, throwing sheets of ice up as they turned and braked.

We started dating. Ron went out of his way to make sure the kids enjoyed his company. He did silly things like taking us out to dinner and, after we were seated, announcing, "Okay, we're all ordering dessert first."

The kids, surprised, said, "What?" and then enjoyed dessert as the first course.

Charlie considered Ron "Goofy" and Ron's son Jeremy, "Cool." At the time, Jeremy was training for the US Junior Olympic ski team and was Rollerblading down a Camelback Mountain road, weaving between cones at high speed. Charlie, of course, had to do the same thing. It was only a matter of time before he was an expert Rollerblader.

Suddenly we were a family. Our dates included the kids, in mostly physical activities such as running, biking, ice skating, and hiking.

Ron and the boys on their bikes, along with me with Adele on the back of my bicycle, rode on the dirt roads along a canal which runs for miles through Phoenix.

On one date we played tennis, with Adele, in diapers, running around picking up the balls for us.

Soon, our relationship grew stronger and, over time, we became much closer. When we started dating, Ron went to church with me. I had one rule: If Ron wanted a serious relationship, he had to go with us to church every Sunday. (He continues to this day, thirty years later.)

One Sunday, we were sitting in church, with Ron holding one of the kids quietly on his lap.

At one point, looking up at the cross, then at Ron, and said, "Mrs. Keating said you are Jewish and you have long hair."

Ron turned and asked, "Did Mrs. Keating say that?"

Ron thought for a moment, and said, "See that guy up on the cross? He's Jewish and Jesus has long hair."

Problem solved.

When people ask Ron how he can go to a Catholic church every Sunday when he isn't even a Catholic, he replies, "Thank you. It's not bad. I think it's a great thing for children to have a sense of appreciation for religion and faith in God. I also think it's important for a family to go to church together, and the Old Testament is usually the first reading."

I always smile at this comment because the Torah, or Hebrew Bible, has the first five Books of our Catholic Bible's Old Testament. We have three readings at Mass and the first is usually from the Old Testament.

Ron knew how important it was to go to church weekly as a family, but didn't understand why I wasn't allowed to receive Communion with the kids. The reason was even though we were married in a civil ceremony two years before, we needed an annulment of our respective marriages by the Catholic Church to allow me to take Communion. Ron thought it was so important to me, that he attended annulment classes monthly for two years, with a nun named Sister Ruth, in Phoenix. He was granted his annulment, and I had mine from the Catholic Church. We were married at St. Joseph Catholic Church by Father Frank Fernandez, in 1996. Ron may not be Catholic, but I am taking Communion with my children and that includes our daughter Ali, who is being raised as a Catholic.

Chapter 10

Stepdad

I was often asked at the grocery store or at parties, "How did you raise a Navy SEAL?"

My response, in jest, was, "I probably was a mean mom or too strict!"

The answer actually was that it was not only up to me, but up to the child and his stepdad ....

During the Florida Orthopedic Society 2018 state meeting, Ron spoke about being a stepparent. He said, "I, of course, was a stepparent. That means from the time the children were ages four, three, and one, I was emotionally, financially, and intellectually the decision maker and a responsible party, but without much authority. I carried a lot of potential clout, though. The ultimate fear and punishment the kids had, when in trouble, was Krista's threat that 'I'll tell Ron!' They did not want to upset Ron!"

One of the first bonding experiences for Ron and Charlie was "Scratchy." When Ron and I started seeing each other, the three children and I often went to visit Ron at his home. The house was much as you would expect for a bachelor orthopedic surgeon: with white wood floors, a nice white couch, modern silver lamps, black marble tables, and everything absolutely spotless. It was an upscale guy's pad.

Whenever the children came in, he'd, understandably, tell them, "Don't touch anything. Be careful. Watch where you're going."

I watched the kids, running after them if they went too close to something fragile or expensive, and fretted that they would mess up the pristine white couch by spilling something on it.

At one point, I even made the comment: "You know, when you die, we are going to bury you on the white couch because then you can take it with you."

Invariably, I suggested we go to the swimming pool or do something where we wouldn't have to worry about Ron's furnishings.

Charlie, who had just started going to school, had been having difficulty reconciling himself with the divorce. He was moody and didn't understand why his parents weren't living in the same house anymore.

Early one evening, we went to a Chinese restaurant which happened to be next to a pet store. Ron could see that Charlie was troubled, and sensed it was because of the divorce.

After we finished eating dinner, Ron said, "Hey, Charlie! Let's go over and look in the window and see what the dogs are doing over there."

He took Charlie and Jeremy over to the window, where they watched a little, black, fluffy, part poodle and part terrier puppy.

The dog stared up at the three of them, and Charlie said, "Oh. Hi!"

The dog rolled over onto his back, and that was all it took.

Ron—who, with his strict German upbringing, had never had a dog, a cat, or even a goldfish for a pet—bought the dog for Charlie on the spot. Even though it was a gift for Charlie, Ron decided to keep it at his home.

We named the dog Scratchy and took it to Ron's house. The cute little, black, fluffy puppy promptly climbed up onto the pristine white couch and peed on it.

I was shocked! Ron was going to be upset! What was he going to do?

Ron's whole demeanor changed instantly. He wasn't upset at all and even chuckled. After that, he was much more relaxed about the children in his house and accepted the fact that accidents happen, children can make a mess, and it's not a big deal.

Later, Charlie, Ron, and the dog would go for runs, often as much as eight miles. Ron's consideration for Charlie helped cement a lifelong friendly relationship.

The greatest thing about Ron, for the kids, was that he provided skills I didn't have. With his son, Jeremy, training to be a competitive skier, the kids naturally learned to ski at a young age. Ron told me how great skiing was for active kids because the boundaries were there, but they had the freedom to explore. Not only did skiing bring us closer as a family, but we also were entertained by the kids' skiing.

Once, when Jeremy was going to participate in a ski race, Ron said, "I bought a ski trainer we can use so Adele can ski with us." A ski trainer is like a long leash that attaches to the beginner skier.

So, Adele started to ski when she was two-and-a-half years old. Ron showed her how to make a turn and how to stop when they started their first run. When Jeremy was starting down the slope in the race, they stopped to watch. Adele began to slide, and Ron, trying to stop her, tripped over the leash.

The two of them rolled down the steep slope while Jeremy whizzed by them, unseen, as they tried to stop rolling. When they finally stopped, unhurt, and found their way back to the slope— Adele laughing all the way—they found that Jeremy had one of his best runs ever and had placed high among the competitors. Ron, covered with snow, stood scanning the area for him, not realizing he was gone!

One time in Mammoth, California, Ron and Jeremy were riding a ski lift when they spotted the kids tearing straight down the steep mountainside, dangerously close to one another. Barreling down the mountain at breakneck speed, they would inevitably crash. One of them decided to take a turn, and the two fell and became two giant snowballs cascading down the mountain. Snow shot up in the air, goggles, ski poles, skis, and miscellaneous debris littered the landscape, as if a truck had plowed through a garage sale. We found out they had tied their ski goggles together with the strings from their ski tickets. They looked like Siamese twins racing down the mountain—until one made an independent decision.

Skiing can be dangerous when getting creative; the boys learned this firsthand. On New Year's Eve 1997, as we were starting a ski run at about two o'clock, we watched two adult skiers tossing a small rubber football back and forth as they skied.

Ron, an expert skier, said, "You don't want to do stuff like that while you're skiing because you could run off the trail or run into a tree or hit somebody."

When we had finished the run and were standing in line to go up to the top of the mountain again, one of the men, in a hurry to get ahead of us, ran right over Charlie's skis and bumped into me as they cut in line in front of us to jump onto the ski lift.

Shortly afterward, when we finished the next run, ambulances appeared, along with the Ski Patrol. One of the men, Michael Kennedy, son of Robert Kennedy, had hit a tree while playing catch with the rubber football. Less than fifteen minutes after one of their group ran over Charlie's skis, Michael Kennedy died. We found out later that this was an activity the Kennedys had practiced for years.

I think all of our children learned an important lesson from this experience, realizing that doing something like that could end your life. I believe Charlie carried that learning experience with him for the rest of his life.

Aspen was the place where the kids could ski in the winter and train for running in the summer. Summer training included running up Aspen Mountain, known as Ajax to the locals. Charlie's record was 35 minutes, which is incredible since the mountain is 11,000 feet. Ron and I take an hour or more to hike it; Charlie ran it!

Something was always going on involving a sports activity of one kind or another. Ron's son was training for the US Ski

Team, and Charlie was the younger brother. After Jeremy made the US Junior Ski Team, he went off to college at Dartmouth.

Charlie was now the oldest at home and looking to his future. Wanting to do well, especially in running, he decided he was going to be the best he possibly could be. He placed in the top ten at state races, but he really wanted to win.

Ron invited his cross-country team and the coach for a training camp in Aspen the summer before Charlie's junior year. The results from an athlete's junior year in high school are what recruiters for college scholarships keep on record. Charlie was determined to train at altitude, lift weights and run double workouts.

The coach told Charlie, "If you do what I ask, without complaining, you will attain your goals."

At the time, Charlie wrote down his goals for the year: "Run a 4:15 mile, 1:56 800 m, make the Junior World Team in steeplechase, and in the off-season, strength training, weights (upper body, core work, stomach), and work with George Young." He added: "Have a grade point average of 3.0."

From the start of this camp, the boys shared camaraderie, cooking, and running up and down the mountain trails. After they left, in terrific shape, Charlie continued his training.

He was training hard, especially in Aspen, during the summer vacation. Ron and Charlie decided to run from the top of the Continental Divide, located northeast of Aspen, along the trail, and into town. Parts of the trail were almost nonexistent, so a local paragliding friend, who knew the trail, went with them.

The three of them took off at six o'clock in the morning, leaving from the top of Independence Pass, which was about twelve thousand feet in altitude. They ran down to Aspen, four thousand feet lower.

Charlie and the guide finished in four hours. Ron, like them, had to fight his way through rough, unmarked parts of the trail, climbing over ridges along the way. Ron was in serious trouble when he ran out of water, but finally finished and got water from me. He completed the trek in six hours.

Upon finishing, Charlie said, "Ah, it was nothing."

Ron, the expert paraglider and champion skater, said, "Really?"

Charlie, at that point, was in such good condition, he could have kept right on running. It was for his junior year that he received scholarship offers from many colleges because he had attained his goals.

As Charlie was maturing and becoming a teenager, Ron felt the need to try to get him talking and relating to him. At the skateboarding park in Aspen, Charlie tried his best at dropping in, gliding, and jumping on his skateboard or even Rollerblades. Ron didn't know how to skate on a skateboard, but he could skate with Rollerblades. He secretly paid a skateboard instructor to teach him how to "drop in" to the skate park on a skateboard. He wanted to show up and drop in with the boys.

When Ron was ready, he padded every part of his body—with a helmet and arm, elbow, wrist, butt, and knee pads—and showed up at the skate park. Adele blushed and rolled her eyes, thinking Ron was going to embarrass Charlie. It was the opposite. Charlie grinned at Ron, watched him drop in, and thought it was the coolest thing ever! He and Ron became even closer, and Charlie showed him how to do other tricks on the skateboard.

Ron was great about noticing Charlie's interests and then following through. Charlie saw a young girl on TV flying an airplane.

He said, "Mom, can I learn to fly a plane?"

I said, "I know you're good at math and you made it through SCUBA instruction, but do you really think you have the courage to fly a plane?"

He answered, "I'll go to flight classes and study every day."

Ron thought it would be a good idea. He arranged for Charlie to earn a student license at Sky Harbor Airport in Phoenix. Charlie loved flying and did well taking off and landing.

Later it turned out that one of the men in his class was interested in flying, but not in landing. This man was one of the 9/11 hijackers.

At one point, when both his grandfather (who had been a Navy pilot) and his father were watching, they noted that Charlie seemed to be a natural at landing a plane.

With his flying, running competitions, and schoolwork, Charlie wasn't able to complete the written training and, although he flew with instructor pilots, he never soloed.

A little later, Ron said, "I have an idea. I'll show you how to paraglide and jump off the top of mountains."

Excited, Charlie said, "What! I'd love to do that!"

Using the skills he had learned from pilot's training and with Ron's tutelage, Charlie quickly became an expert at takeoffs and landings while paragliding in Aspen.

Ron's influence lasted throughout Charlie's life. One college entrance application requirement was to write an essay in the third person. Charlie chose to write about Ron, his stepdad.

The paper was written in 2003, by Charles Keating IV:

> Bad things happen in series. And the Keatings had the world series of bad things in the early '90s. Charles II was in prison in the savings and loan scandal, Charles III had been jailed on charges stemming from the scandal and a very frightened preschool Charles IV was watching his parents get divorced—and the world as he knew it disappear. (Note: Charges against Charles III were eventually dismissed, according to the Washington Post.)
>
> In the blink of an eye, the family went from dining with royalty and saints and living in splendor, to barely managing to survive. The new home was a small house on loan from my maternal grandparents. Meals were scarce. The government seized all the assets—including the business, which had employed everyone including my

mother.

Still, there were some bright spots. My maternal grandparents had a cabin in Mexico, and me and my siblings went there as frequently as we could. There, at least, life had not altered so radically, food was plentiful—and there was plenty to do to keep small children from wondering and worrying about things that were way out of their control.

It was after one of the trips to Mexico that Ron came into our lives. More accurately, the former Olympian barged into our lives. His opening gambit was a slew of gifts that appeared at the front door. A boogie board, squirt guns, and candy.

"Who is this guy? And why all the neat stuff?"

Mom sighed. "Okay," she said, "his name is Ron, and he has been sending flowers and calling every day for a month."

"Where'd he come from?" Six-year-olds ask the darnedest questions.

"It's complicated. But this weirdo saw me at a restaurant, finagled a phone number from a friend, and ...."

The rest was history. It was probably the dog that did it. The one he got me for no better reason than I said that I wanted one. The way to a woman's heart obviously is through her kids.

They were married five years later—the joke being that my mother stayed true to form—marrying an Olympian again. My father was an Olympic swimmer, and Ron took bronze in pairs figure skating.

He really has been larger than life—an Olympian medaling in fatherhood. It was Ron who had the patience, love, and generosity of spirit to walk into a house with three kids—three kids whose world had collapsed—and take them under his wing. It was Ron who convinced me to take up skiing, backpacking, and hiking. It was Ron who insisted that we all come along wherever my brother, a world-class skier, was competing.

"How else are you going to learn about other cultures?"

Of course, once we came along, we got sucked in to trying everything. Paragliding, rock climbing, mountain biking.

"All of these skills serve you well."

It is Ron who stands by the finish line waiting for me—even if he has to change his schedule to be there. It is Ron who encourages me to get back on the track after a crushing defeat. It is Ron who celebrates when I win a race.

So, while bad things might occur in a series, good things arrive individually. Or they arrive, as did Ron, in a whirlwind—as a gift from the gods."

Finding this essay in my filing cabinet was such a blessing. It shows how much a stepfather truly matters in a blended family. A stepdad can provide children with stability, strength, and new adventures. Most importantly, the love between a husband and a wife forms a family bond.

I love that by finding his essay, I was able to "hear" from Charlie and what he thought about his life, growing up.

Chapter 11

Golden Boy

I don't know what it was, but Charlie was the "golden boy." He was lucky.

His grandfather used to say, "Luck favors the brave."

I'm not sure if it was Charlie's huge smile, his mischievous blue eyes, his positive attitude, or his drive, but he was always lucky.

As a nine-year-old boy, he called us on the phone and, in his little voice, said, "Mom! I lost my wallet!"

He was at the Air Force Academy where he was participating in their summer two-week track and field program. We were staying in Denver, not too far away, and planned to pick him up after the program ended. Two days later, his wallet showed up.

If there was a Phoenix Suns basketball game where T-shirts were being thrown at the audience, we could be in the "nose-bleed section" and see Charlie, on the floor, receiving one from a cheerleader.

When he was twelve years old, he was traveling on a United Airlines plane. He put his prized collection of twenty CDs in the pouch of the seat in front of him and forgot them when he left the plane.

I told him, "You're never going to see them again!"

Back at home, he phoned everyone he could possibly talk to at United Airlines. He told them what seat he was in, what flight he was on. Charlie was persistent. When his first attempt was unproductive, he called again and spoke with someone else. Then he wrote them a letter with the same details.

Sure enough, three weeks later, a package with his CDs showed up at our door.

One time, when he was older, a FedEx package came to us from a well-known person. Charlie had left his wallet in a rental car. All of his money and the credit cards were still there. This type of thing happened many times, and always ended happily.

In July 1996, we had driven across from Arizona to Atlanta to attend the Summer Olympics in Atlanta. Ron and I were sitting with the kids, with about a thousand other people between us and the stage, watching Sinbad the comedian-actor on the Jumbotron. He was on the stage behind the Olympic Plaza. We had spread out a blanket to sit on. Soon after the show started, I looked up and noticed Charlie missing.

I said, "Where's Charlie?"

Adele answered, "He went to the bathroom."

Before we knew it we saw eleven-year-old Charlie on the Jumbotron, talking with Sinbad, who was very popular at that time. We didn't even know Charlie had left and never did figure out how he found his way there.

We learned how to ride the MARTA (Metropolitan Rapid Atlanta Transit Authority) subway in Atlanta. The subway was a convenient way to go back and forth to the Centennial Olympic Park from our hotel, which was near the subway station. We didn't have a problem letting the children ride back to our hotel by themselves, as long as Nicholas, an older boy who had come with us, was with them. At the time of the Olympics, Atlanta security was at its peak and the MARTA was almost empty.

One day, when it started to get late, we wanted to go back to the hotel, but the boys wanted to stay a little longer. Ron, Adele, and I went back to the hotel, and the others joined us about an hour later.

We were settled in and turned on the television, only to hear the news that a bomb had exploded almost exactly where we had been sitting. A man named Eric Robert Rudolph had set off a pipe bomb that killed one person and injured 111 others. Charlie's luck again—or intuition—had brought him safely to the hotel.

We accompanied Charlie to his favorite concerts when he was in middle school. Ron and I went to Korn, Smashing Pumpkins, and, yes, Kid Rock. Little did we know Charlie had made his way from our seats and was crowd surfing at all of them.

Charlie's younger sister was going to have a party on her thirteenth birthday, attending a concert by Belinda Carlisle and the Go-Go's, but the singer canceled because she had a sore throat. Unfortunately, we had not heard this. The eight girls and I packed into the car, dressed up like the Go-Go's, and arrived at the venue to find no cars! You should have seen their disappointment, so I took them to a nice restaurant where they had ice cream, and Adele opened presents.

I called the ticket office and told them we had front row seats to the Go-Go's for my daughter's birthday party and they were devastated when they got there and found out it had been canceled. The ticket office offered me front row seats to a Billy Idol concert to make up for the cancellation.

I thought, *I liked Billy Idol when I was younger. He isn't much like the Go-Go's, but, yeah, I'll take those tickets.*

I gave the tickets to Charlie, Adele, and some of their friends. They researched Billy Idol on the Internet and found that he wore a leather vest and had tattoos, so Charlie put on a leather vest and fake tattoos. The group went down and sat in the front row of the theatre among the other patrons, most of whom were in their forties.

Charlie loved dressing up and becoming someone else. Every year at his elementary school in Phoenix, Alice Cooper (rocker) and his wife Cheryl put on a talent show for charity. The kids were part of the show. Sometimes Charlie was the "goof" and other times the satirical comedian. The "Keating kids" were always together in a skit, until they graduated one by one, and Adele had a skit by herself. Later in life, Charlie dressed up in high school, college, and … yes, as Rambo, when he was a Navy SEAL.

The program started. Billy Idol came in and began playing his music. When he started playing one of his trademark songs, "Dancing with Myself," Charlie started dancing with himself, at the same time making the classic Billy Idol chin-up nod.

Charlie stood up in front of the stage, pointed at Billy Idol, and, dancing with himself, made eye contact. Billy Idol responded by pointing at Charlie. Billy Idol started singing to him and with him.

Charlie, of course, made a point to sing Idol's "White Wedding" song to Adele, with the lyrics, "Hey little sister, what have you done?"

Charlie's friends were yelling, and the crowd went wild. After the concert, Billy Idol gave Charlie a drumstick, which joined another drumstick from the Korn concert, as a souvenir.

Many years later, as a SEAL, he often wore a Billy Idol T-shirt under his armored vest in Afghanistan, for luck.

Another opportunity opened up for Charlie when I saw an article about a TV program named *Outward Bound*. They were scouting for fourteen-year-old kids to try out for the Discovery Channel's show. The article described how a group of eight teenagers would learn how to survive in the wilderness under the guidance of instructors. The show was unrehearsed and shot at various locations around the world.

I knew Charlie would be interested since he loved to watch the television show, *Survivor*, and Charlie's other favorite show was about a man who went into the wilderness with minimum equipment and survived by eating berries, trapping squirrels, and using his wits. Charlie was good-looking, smart, and funny, so it seemed like it would be a real adventure for him.

I signed him up to try out for the show. When I told Charlie what I did, and they wanted a video, his response was a huge grin and "Let's start filming!"

We made a video showing him working out with his track

coach. It also showed him with a bow and arrow, going around our property like he was hunting for food to survive. Next, it showed him falling into the swimming pool with his clothes on. He talked about himself. He didn't have stage fright and was impressive. He was creative and funny.

We sent the video in, but I didn't think he would make the show. One day, though, I received a phone call.

A woman said, "We'd like to meet him in person in Phoenix."

I was surprised. "Really?" I said.

"Yes. We are meeting a lot of kids and we would like to meet him. This is for an episode in Australia. Do you think he can travel alone and not get homesick for a month?"

I replied, "Are you kidding me? He would love to get away from his brothers and sisters."

So, we went to the interview. Charlie was at his best! He looked her in the eye, smiled his huge grin, and talked continuously.

The woman in charge of casting called me a few days later and said, "Gosh! I really like him, but we didn't pick him. I'm going to put his information in a file because, you never know, maybe for the next show."

I thought, *Oh, it's over. I'll never hear from them again.*

Two weeks later she called again and said, "We've picked him for the Costa Rica episode. Can he go?" She asked again if he was going to be homesick.

I said, "No. We went to track meets all over the country, and he has traveled outside of the country since he was a baby. He's an experienced traveler. He'll be great."

When I drove to pick him up after school, I will never forget his face when I told him he had made the television show. We both hugged and cheered in the front seat of the car. He was so happy.

I remember when Charlie was six or seven years old. We often visited my parents' one-room place on the beach in Mexico.

It was, in fact, camping; it was, literally, one room with a kitchen. Charlie loved sleeping in the hammock at night, to wake up with the sunrise. He played with the Mexican children his age, even though they didn't speak the same language. Charlie gathered a group of boys and girls to play soccer, build sandcastles, and eat lunch. We drove him to town and gave him five dollars to see how big an item he could bargain for in the Mexican markets. Of course, Charlie came out on top and made a few friends at the same time!

The only issue about going to Costa Rica—besides missing school—was that he was starting to become a very good runner and the time frame of the show's filming was during school, right before track season. We thought this would interfere with his training. However, he was only a freshman in high school and would still have three more years to compete.

We cleared it with the school so Charlie could make up the work he'd miss. He prepared to go to Costa Rica.

Charlie and I knew *Outward Bound* had an overnight challenge; they would spend a night by themselves in the wilderness. I told him to do something funny when he spent the night alone so they would have a good clip for the TV show.

Charlie flew from Phoenix to San Jose, Costa Rica, on February 17, 2001. Eager to start the new adventure, he complained that the flight over was too long and boring. There, he was met by the *Outward Bound* staff and the other teenage boys and girls in their group, for the start of a fourteen-day adventure of a lifetime.

He said, "As soon as we arrived, the cameras were in my face." The filming of the show began before he was out of the airport.

When getting acquainted, Charlie discovered that the other teenagers were from all over the country. They, of course, had never met. Because they had been specially selected, he understood that their common bond was the expectation to successfully experience the difficult and exciting times they were about to face. This meant they had to be both physically fit, mentally capable, and emotionally stable. The hope was to bring the kids together as a team.

After a long bus ride, they were taken to their temporary quarters. They were briefed, and the kids spent the rest of the day making friends, talking, and preparing for their first adventure. They were told they had to leave everything behind, even their names. They then chose names, among which were Estrella, Tiger, Fuego, Zorro, Sloth, and Ave. Charlie became Choncho because it meant "pig" in Spanish. I'm sure Charlie picked the name because of his enormous appetite.

He was a skinny boy who ran a lot. While he was at school, there was a Pizza Hut next to the school's twelve-foot fence. In retrospect, I'd say it was a great deal for Pizza Hut and not such a good one for the high school students. Charlie was extra hungry one day and scrambled up the chain-link fence. The security guard noticed and, in his golf cart, drove over to the Pizza Hut, following Charlie. As Charlie was finishing his order, the security guard was right behind him and tapped him on the shoulder. Of course, with a large grin and his twinkling eyes, Charlie offered him part of his pizza. Charlie never was punished by the school, but Mom found out!

He soon became friends with Sloth, and told us, "He was my best friend on the trip." It seemed these two were just as mischievous, athletic, and fun-loving as the other.

Unfortunately, one of the girls was always complaining. Charlie was not a fan of complainers and was hoping for excitement and adventure. He knew that complaining would not help the group as a team.

He often said, "Do everything 150 percent!"

They woke up at six the following day, and after breakfast—at which they ate snake—they went into the center of San Jose to learn about the local culture and see for themselves how people lived in this Central American country. They were impressed by the noisy, congested traffic with small cars and trucks, and the bicycles and scooters darting through the city. Then they were interviewed by the staff for the TV program. Charlie's footage on the program was of him eating and dripping mango juice, as well as getting stuck in the bus door. Perfect for Choncho. When they returned to their quarters, they were issued the equipment they would need for the adventure.

Charlie's comment was, "A day without brothers or sisters! Yay!"

The next two days, they were introduced to everything they had expected: thrills, physical demands, and exhilaration. One of the staff members, an expert at rafting, instructed the teenagers on how to use the rafts, helmets, paddles, and so on. Charlie quickly became friends with the man who led them to successfully paddle a rubber raft while carrying all eight of them down a wild, tortuous whitewater river in the jungles of Costa Rica.

Charlie exclaimed, "Whitewater rafting was so much fun! We went on Class Two and some Class Three rapids!"

The next day, they did even more difficult whitewater rafting, tackling Class Four rapids.

I received a phone call later, informing me Charlie was okay.

It's hard when you hear the first thing out of the producer's mouth, "Charlie's okay, but he was dumped into the river from the raft."

I was told the only reason they called was because it would be shown on the TV episode and they wanted to make sure I knew he was all right. When watching the scene later, I saw it was dangerous and, luckily, he thought fast. When he was thrown over, he grabbed at the side and secured one of the ropes. He hung on for dear life until they were out of the rapids. I thank God he didn't hit one of the boulders.

Charlie said, "Today was great! I and a girl named Estrella both fell off the raft. I nailed my back on a rock, but I wasn't badly hurt. All in all, it was an amazing experience!"

After this experience, he wrote a note to me, saying, "I miss you! A lot! I'm giving you a thought hug."

A few weeks after the adventure ended, we got a call from

Outward Bound, informing us that the man, Rio, who had taught and led the group on the whitewater trips, had drowned in the same river while leading another group with their kayaks. Charlie was visibly touched by his death. The producers dedicated the show to the man when it aired on the Discovery Channel that summer.

When the second episode was shown on TV, there was a special segment featuring Charlie, titled, "Choncho Mania." Even though all the members of the group were selected as specially qualified for this adventure, Charlie had already emerged as a leader within the group on the first two days of *Outward Bound.*

They hiked for an hour-and-a-half one day, to a rocky cliff where they first climbed the rock and then rappelled it, under the tutelage of the staff. Charlie was the first of the group to be able to climb the more difficult passage to the top of the rock. Others in the group followed, using the same passageway he had used.

One thing he told me when he came home: "I had to pull myself up to the top of the mountain three times. The cameraman wanted a better shot!"

One day, the teenagers were guests at a home in the rain forest. They spent a day and a night at the primitive home while chickens and pigs ran around the area. After sleeping outside on the rudimentary porch, on the following day they went to visit another family, also in the rain forest. This time, the home was larger, but still primitive. The family there had young children and the group enjoyed playing with them and learning about local customs. They feasted on "wild beast"—otherwise known as jungle rat, a large rodent-type animal. Of course, we watched this later; the little toddlers were climbing over Charlie as he tickled and played with them and made funny noises. The kids were yelling "Choncho, Choncho," and were giggling with delight!

While there, they went into the jungle and explored a cave at a place named Piedras Blancas, or White Rocks. They descended along the narrow, muddy, slippery trail with their infrared lights so they could see where they were going. They could see bats flying around and spiders crawling along the way. When they reached the bottom of the cave, the instructors told them they would now go back without using the infrared lights. This meant they had to hand the lights to the instructors, after which the instructors left.

Within a few minutes—when the kids realized their predicament—Charlie said, "Okay, everyone. I'll lead the way. Grab each other's hands. We'll make a chain and work together."

Slowly, Charlie, my future Navy SEAL, feeling his way along the wall of the cave, led the group back up through the dark, eerie cave. The video photographers, with night vision goggles, were the only people left with the group, but they were not allowed to communicate. Finally, they saw daylight as they approached the entrance to the cave. The chain of kids had broken up farther down the line and they were not happy when they eventually made their way out.

Sloth and Charlie went with one of their hosts to help clear the area around banana trees. Using machetes, they cut the weeds around the plants. This had to be done every two months to grow good crops of bananas. Not used to swinging a machete, Charlie got blisters on his hands, yet loved using the big "sword." He felt like he was right out of the movie *Rambo*. I still have his machete today because he gave it to Ron as a birthday present.

Then came the day when they'd spend twenty-four hours alone in the woods. The campers each had their own video camera, and Charlie made the best of it. He acted out the entire *Blair Witch Project*, imitated *Pet Detective*, and drew his name, Choncho, and a picture of a pig on the giant leaves surrounding his tent. After getting bored at nightfall, Charlie and Sloth had decided to tease the other campers during the night. In their separate areas, the two made strange, loud, wild animal noises and screamed to alarm the instructors. The instructors came running with medical kits—and panic on their faces. Charlie gave his best, "I don't know what you are talking about face" while his friend continued screaming, unaware of the counselors headed his way. Sloth got caught; Charlie got away with the prank. The two instructors yelled at Sloth, and you can see Charlie laughing hysterically in the background.

The next day they went to the Savegre River. The girl who complained had not participated the previous day and wanted to rejoin the group. There was some resentment among the others because she had left earlier and had been a hindrance to the group. They had a discussion and, with Charlie acting as one of the leaders, established guidelines for her to rejoin.

Charlie reminded them, "We all have to give 150 percent effort to this experience."

(He was wearing a USMC T-shirt given to him by his stepbrother, Jeremy, who, along with sixteen other Ivy League graduates, all athletes, joined the Marines in late 2000 and early 2001.)

We had often used this 150 percent line in other things Charlie did, partly as a joke, but in reality, everything he did physically was his best effort *plus*. Unfortunately, he did not always apply the same effort to some of his schoolwork!

Their final challenge was at Rancho Tranquillo, along the coast. Teamwork was again needed as the group constructed a raft by pumping up three-foot inflatable bags and tying them together to form a raft. Their first attempt failed; their raft flipped over and fell apart soon after they boarded it and tried to paddle away.

Charlie, again, was one of the leaders who directed the rebuilding of the raft. The group then successfully paddled the raft across the river to the other shore.

Soon after they arrived, they were given letters from home, their first outside contact since they had joined the group twelve days earlier. His letter from home contained jelly beans from me. He told me later that he really appreciated the candy in the wilderness! That night they slept on the Playa Savegre beach and the following day rafted back to the other side.

Their final day, the group had a graduation ceremony. Some of the teenagers presented others, who had shown leadership, with primitive necklaces. Charlie was presented with one for "keeping the group happy."

One of the instructors said, "He enjoyed himself all the time."

Fuego, one of the teenagers, said, "He has the biggest smile I've ever seen."

The next day, the members of the group, now friends, went their separate ways and Charlie returned to Arizona.

Charlie was ecstatic about his adventure. Some of his comrades on the expedition had expressed their desire to become actors or models.

He said, "I could be a model. I spoke to all the people involved in the show and the cameramen. I got to know them, and I really think I should try this modeling and acting thing."

Of course, I knew these were sedentary jobs. You sit around and wait, and they take your pictures. I was sure Charlie would be successful if he did that because he resembled Ashton Kutcher and had the personality that would make him successful.

But I said to him, "Is that what you want to do for the world, just be a pretty face and be in pictures? It would drive you crazy to sit around and wait. Or do you want to do something in the world that means something?"

I knew he wanted to be a Navy SEAL, even though it wasn't something he talked about all the time. I remember Charlie as a young boy of seven, he hung a SEAL poster over his bed because it was the toughest thing anyone could do.

I said, "Is being a model going to be enough for you in your life? Isn't it going to be a boring job?

While he didn't say much in response, I could see he was thinking, and it wasn't long before he went back to his original plan—to become a Navy SEAL.

Watching the TV program gave me a great opportunity to see how my son would act when he was away from his family. While he was invariably polite and respectful and usually followed rules, this program let me see that he acted the same way when he was away from me and our home. I was proud of the way he handled himself during these experiences. He was funny, hungry, and creative. His athletic ability stood out, especially when they were doing physical things like rock climbing and whitewater rafting. Most of all, I have a ten-episode video to view, where I can watch Charlie for the rest of my life.

With his good fortune always following him, it seemed he would attain anything he set his mind to.

Chapter 12

College

Charlie's luck held out at the end of high school. He had been training hard to obtain a scholarship. He had already placed 2nd in state, running a 4:17, 1600 meter (approximately a mile). Several colleges were watching his final senior year.

Charlie was scheduled to run in a school meet way out in north Scottsdale one evening. One of the competitors was a rival who had always beat Charlie in previous races.

As we were preparing to go, it was pouring rain.

I said, "Oh, Charlie. It's way out in north Scottsdale at Desert Mountain. The meet's going to be canceled with this rain."

We had planned to go separately, and he said, "No, I'm going to go. I'll meet you there."

I reluctantly agreed, thinking, *Another meet we'll be sitting in the rain and he will have a good performance, but will lose to this superstar that he has lost to before.*

When we arrived at Desert Mountain, the rain had stopped. The air was crisp and the weather was perfect for the meet. Ron and I were sitting in the stands. While we were waiting for his race, Charlie was acting funny, running up and down the steps. He put his red, white, and blue bandana tied around his forehead, his Navy SEAL T-shirt over his uniform, and was talking with some girls and goofing off, throwing some bags around with another teammate.

I called him over. "Charlie," I said, "we drove all the way

out here. You're not taking this seriously. If we had known you weren't going to take it seriously, we would have stayed home."

He said, "Watch me, Mother!"

I thought, *Oh, really. Oh my God.*

When it came time for his race, we went up into the stands to watch as they lined up to run the 800-meter race (two laps around the track). He ran the first lap with the pack of runners, but as they started the second and final lap of the race, he took off running fifteen meters in front of the pack.

At this point, his competitor realized Charlie wasn't going to drop back, so he ran hard and was able to pull up near Charlie. That motivated Charlie even more and, with a hundred meters to go, Charlie, with a burst of speed, pulled farther ahead and won the race.

They both hugged after the race and became good friends.

After the race, I thought, *Thank God I went! I might have talked Charlie out of going and we would never have had this fantastic experience.*

Charlie later competed in a well-attended Nationals-caliber race in Chandler, Arizona, called the Chandler Rotary. Every athlete who placed first would win a watch, which made it a cool meet. Charlie ran in the mile race, leading all the way until the last hundred yards, when he fell behind and, even though he ran the mile in four minutes and twenty seconds, he still got beat. Charlie did not like to lose, and he was trying to better his 4:17 mile time.

He still had to run the 800-meter race an hour later.

I thought, *Gosh, after that disappointing mile, he's running against an out-of-state champion runner who has won races across the country, including the Nationals. I just hope Charlie gets a good time.*

The announcer introduced the kid who was the champion and a list of his accomplishments.

The runners started off with the favorite runner leading all the way.

I thought, *He's well-known for this and has won many important races.*

The announcer kept talking about the boy, like a commentary on television, while he was running—how great he was and where he was going to college.

All at once, Charlie did what he had done in the earlier race at the Desert Mountain school. He put on a burst of speed near the end and won the race.

The announcer was astonished and stuttered for a moment before he recovered and said, "Whoa! That was Charlie Keating running a 1:52!" Another one of those perfect moments I'm glad I was there to see. Charlie was so proud of himself and finally won a coveted watch.

Charlie was a fairly good student in grade school, but he fell behind in middle school and high school. It was clear he would rather be doing other things than reading, unless it was something he was particularly interested in. He had a tremendous drive to excel in anything he was interested in, like physics, math, guns, or the Navy SEALs. At the same time, other things like English grammar turned him off and he performed poorly.

His high school grades in French were poor, but he needed to pass to compete in his final state track meet. He didn't understand why he needed to take French. However, later, in college, he signed up to study Swahili, which is found only in three African countries and wasn't even a written language until 1928.

But in French, when he had done so poorly on a test that he had to retake it, he convinced his French teacher that he had studied hard but wouldn't be able to run in the track meet if he didn't get a passing grade.

I found out later, after Charlie ran in the State meet, he had talked to his teacher *on his knees* and asked, "What can I help you with? Is there something? I could make a sign for you for French class, so that I can pass?" I'm glad I did not know this until later in his life.

With less than two months of high school left, and after Charlie had already committed to attend the University of Indiana on a cross-country scholarship, I was alone at home one night. The kids were visiting at their father's house for the weekend. Ron had gone to perform surgeries in Kingman, Arizona, two hundred miles away, and was spending the night there.

The Scottsdale police called me at three o'clock in the morning. Charlie had been in an automobile accident. He wasn't hurt, but he was involved. It had never occurred to me that Charlie might be drinking, and I didn't think he would jeopardize his scholarship at Indiana by going to parties where alcohol was served.

I jumped into my car and headed right over to the site of the accident.

I found out Charlie and his friends had gone to a party and then decided to go to another party down the street. Charlie told me a fifteen-year-old boy from a prominent Phoenix family had been driving our car. When the car hit a speed bump, he hit the brake. A girl who was following them to the next party was driving a Chevrolet Suburban and hit our car from behind.

A police officer told me, "Your son said he wasn't drinking. He said, 'Breathalyzer me. I'm not drinking. Go ahead. Do it. Do it. Breathalyzer me!' So, I did. He registered point one eight, more than twice the legal limit."

I was furious! My first instinct was to teach my son a lesson and let him deal with it.

I told the police officer, "Go ahead and arrest him. Put him in the back seat of your patrol car."

Charlie was shook up, and said, "But I wasn't driving! I didn't even drive. I wasn't even in the front seat."

The officer turned to me and said, "Well, the funny thing is that he told me a fifteen-year-old, who didn't have a license, was driving. It's also bizarre that kids from two prominent families were in the same car. Nobody was hurt. When I got to the car, no one was in the front seat, so I don't know who was driving. The girl who was driving the car that hit yours has an athletic scholarship and she doesn't want to lose that. Her family has agreed to pay for the damage."

By this time, I had calmed down. The only damage to our car was a scratch on the back bumper, although the other car had more serious damage. We let it go, and everyone went to their homes.

Charlie told us much later he would never drive when he had been drinking, so he had talked the fifteen-year-old boy, who hadn't been drinking, into driving, even though he didn't have a license. When the car stopped and got hit from behind, they were right near the boy's house. The boy panicked, jumped out of the car, and ran into his house, leaving Charlie to explain the situation.

This was the first of many times that Charlie was faced with a situation where he could have lost everything. Yet, he always was able to come out of bad situations unscathed. He seemed to have a charmed life and we thought of him as the "golden boy" of the family.

Charlie's life starting college seemed to stay with the trajectory to become a SEAL. When we first brought Charlie to the University of Indiana to start college, Ron and I, while hoping our children would abstain from sex, realized that would likely not happen, so we decided to give him a package of condoms, just in case. We delivered the condoms to him in his new dorm room before we said goodbye.

He took the pack of condoms, said, "Thanks, Mom," and stuck a pin right through the middle of the package, pinning them to the wall above his bed.

Ron's parting comments to Charlie were, "Make sure you study. This girl you're seeing seems nice, but that guy you're hanging out with seems like an idiot. Use your best judgment."

When we went back a few months later, the condoms were still pinned to the wall.

By the time he was in his sophomore year, he was having difficulties with time management and his grades were marginal.

Charlie was doing some great running, but was struggling with his academics.

His girlfriend at the time was helping him with his studies. As a sophomore, he decided to take an art class because he needed a passing grade so he could continue running on the track and cross-country teams. He received a D in the art class, even though the art project he submitted had been done mostly by his girlfriend.

At about the same time, he ran a 1500-meter race in a time equivalent to running a mile in less than four minutes.

He made up his mind, called me, and said, "Mom, I'm done. I'm in the best shape of my life, and I'm going to BUD/S. I'm going to be a Navy SEAL."

BUD/S is the acronym for Basic Underwater Demolition/ SEAL training. It is the first stage of becoming a SEAL.

Ron and I discussed it with him. I asked, "Charlie, how can you do this? You love IU."

Charlie answered, "I really don't want to be here. I'm going to be a SEAL."

When Charlie announced he was going to leave to become a Navy SEAL, his coach said, "What if you die? Why would you go when you might die?"

Charlie responded, "If I die, it will be with honor and I will be dying for my country."

Ron and I felt horrible about this decision. Yet we knew he'd always wanted to be a Navy SEAL. We also realized that, at least at this point in his life, he was not going to be successful in college. We worried he might never go back to college and, if he wasn't successful in SEAL training, he'd end up without a job to support himself. On a different note, he was so charismatic, I was sure he could be successful selling ice cream to Eskimos, if that was what he wanted to do.

Coach Chapman said later to a reporter, "When Charlie left Indiana University to enlist and try to become a SEAL, I don't think it surprised any of us. You could tell he was a guy who wanted to be the best and find out what he was made of, and serving in special operations forces for his country embodied that."

As in Bloomington, Indiana, at a bar called Nick's English Hut, inscribed by Charlie, as a sophomore, on the wall in permanent marker: CHARLES HUMPHREY KEATING, IV, IU MILER, HOPEFULLY SEAL.

Chapter 13

Skills to Be a Navy SEAL?

In high school, there was the day that changed our lives forever. No one wants to forget 9/11. I remember that morning. I was coaching the Arcadia High School cross-country team and we had just finished a cross-country workout.

Charlie was heading to his car, and one of the other runners screamed, "We're under attack! Planes are hitting buildings and the Pentagon!"

Charlie's face was visibly upset and he wanted to go home as soon as possible. We watched in horror, from our living room, as the buildings fell. The air around us became eerily quiet and stayed that way for a week. I think that was the day when paintball and laser tag became more to Charlie than fun. He wanted to be a SEAL.

My son was dropping out of college to try to do one of the hardest things on the planet—become a Navy SEAL. This was quite stressful for me and I was worried he wouldn't make it. I considered the skills he possessed that would help him be successful. When Charlie was thirteen, my father gave him scuba lessons and he became proficient at diving. He was comfortable in the water, especially surfing. He could paraglide, ski, skate, and rock climb. He was a great runner and steeplechaser. The steeplechase skill was the one Charlie ended up using in order to save lives in which he received the Bronze Star Medal with Combat V for Valor in Afghanistan.

The steeplechase is a 3000-meter race involving obstacles similar to those used in track and field hurdles, except these do not collapse when hit by a runner, and runners can use any means to go over the hurdles. Some runners will step on top of them. There is a water pit behind one of the barriers to further challenge the racers.

The sport was becoming popular around 2003–2004, and Charlie started showing a lot of talent in it. For Christmas we bought him a steeple (hurdle), which we put up on the track at his high school, giving him and others the opportunity to practice.

One of our good friends, George Young, was a silver medalist in the steeplechase at the Mexico City Olympics in 1968, so we called and asked him to help train Charlie. (As a young girl I had met George when I was running, and he was training for the Olympics. At our introduction I had him sign my shoe. Later, when I was in high school, I attended a running camp where he was one of the coaches. We have been friends ever since.)

I explained to George that Charlie was small for his age, but was starting to grow. George agreed to our request, and Charlie and I went to the college called Central Arizona, in Casa Grande. Many athletes were being coached here to prepare for the Olympics.

Charlie qualified to run in the USA Junior Nationals, where the meet was at Stanford when he was sixteen. He ran with the top Juniors in the country, placing in the top twenty.

Charlie's skills also included shooting. I taught all my children to shoot when they were young. Living in Phoenix allowed us to go into the desert and shoot at targets. There were also gun ranges. I thought it was important that they know how to handle a firearm. This led to Charlie being on a championship paintball team in high school, which led to the best Mother's Day present ever.

C4 drove up in his dark green Denali and told the entire family to get in the car. I was curious.

He said, "It's Mother's Day, and I'm taking you to your

present!"

I thought, *Well, maybe lunch as a family at the Ritz?* I wasn't dressed up, but looked nice enough.

As we pulled up to a giant metal building, Adele, Ron, and Charlie started laughing. They waited to see if I would go in. It was a paintball arena. Charlie had scheduled our family to a duel. Of course, girls against boys.

Charlie was so excited, with a huge smile on his face and a little drool on the corners of his mouth (this happened when he got excited). That look warmed my heart. I was not going to say no.

I retrieved my equipment and put as much padding and protectors on as possible, like Ron did when skateboarding. I knew it would hurt if I was hit with the paintball. There I was, with Adele, hiding behind a pillar, putting my gun to the side and firing. As I spotted the boys heading our way, Adele and I tried to run for cover behind another wall. She made it, and I, let's say, dove, and every piece of equipment I had on went flying all over the arena.

The referee regarded me lying on the floor and smirked. "Wow," he commented, "never seen that before."

Best Mother's Day ever!

The most important skill C4 had, when I look back, was maintaining the relationship between brothers. If you make it to a SEAL Team, camaraderie is so important. You can still be dropped from a Team if you can't get along with the other Team "brothers." This is where experience with having to get along with a sibling was so important.

The kids always seem to be best buddies—even though they often argued and fought, as kids do—they still would come up with creative things to do. One of their favorites was what they called "Bee on a leash." They would hunt for a bee and sneak up on it and catch it between two Styrofoam cups. They put it in the freezer for a couple of minutes, until the bee was stunned and unable to fly. They tied a string around the bee, and when the bee recovered and started flying, they paraded around with their "bee on a leash." When they tired of this sport, they released the bee.

Another creative moment with SEAL potential involved our swimming pool. There were a lot of large boulders on the side of the desert mountain where we lived. One day I found some giant boulders in the swimming pool. I thought the rocks must have rolled down the mountainside and into the pool. I called an engineer to find out how this was happening and what we could do to stop them from going into the pool.

The engineer checked the area to ensure the boulders on the mountainside were not in a precarious position. He assured me that no more boulders would be coming down the hill. A couple of weeks later, there they were again, in the bottom of the pool.

Many years later, as the kids were laughing and joking about their childhood, they told me they had brought the boulders down and put them in the pool so they could walk underwater, using the boulders to weigh them down while they held breath-holding contests. As a parent, this is not something I would have approved.

Another funny goal was, at one point, when Charlie was adamant to get in the Arcadia High School yearbook. He started a bottle cap league. They used orange Gatorade bottle caps to play a type of water bottle baseball, called Arcadia Bottle Cap Baseball. They developed a league and eventually had a picture taken and placed in the team section of the yearbook. I have never heard of this sport again!

Charlie and his friends came up with an idea to train by running through the sewer system under the city of Phoenix, to the Scottsdale city library, more than six miles away *underground*. They found a small opening at one of the entrances. The only way out of the system was to go back where they had entered. They ran almost twelve miles each time, roundtrip. This ended after they became acquainted with some homeless people who apparently were living in the tunnel. They got along with these people, but noticed the floor of their hideaway was getting dirty.

It appeared they were using it for more things than sleeping.

Charlie seemed to have the skills. Still, I was nervous and perplexed. How was he going to prepare to become a SEAL, without a job? He moved to Coronado and went to see the Navy recruiter, where the Navy gave a guarantee that when he went into the Navy, he'd immediately be sent to the Great Lakes Naval Training Center for basic training and, afterward, go to BUD/S training at Coronado, California. Under the terms of his enlistment, he would receive a bonus of $40,000 if he completed all the SEAL training.

But there was a problem. Charlie could easily run the mile with time to spare. Running the obstacle course, doing push-ups, sit-ups, and the other physical requirements would not be a problem. He had, however, talked with several men who had completed SEAL training and was told that if a candidate had past surgeries, that might disqualify him from joining the SEALs.

Charlie had a medical problem. When he was sixteen years old, he had gall bladder surgery and had surgery for a hernia. His SEAL advisors told him that if he reported these surgeries, he would likely not be accepted in SEAL training.

He was faced with a dilemma. Admit he had those surgeries and take a chance of not being admitted to SEAL training. If he didn't report them, essentially lying, and the scars were discovered, he could still lose out on his lifetime ambition of becoming a Navy SEAL.

He didn't want to lie, but he reluctantly decided that not reporting the surgeries was his best bet. When he had his SEAL physical, the doctor examined his stomach and obviously noticed the small scars but didn't say anything.

Charlie passed his physical.

One last moment could have prevented Charlie from becoming a SEAL. Before he was to report to the Navy and be flown to the Great Lakes, Charlie and one of his friends went to Europe for a few days, on a "last" civilian trip. He had always wanted to travel to Europe as an adult, because as a toddler he could hardly remember his time there.

One day they were on a train in Germany when he and his friend were in the last car. At one of the stops, some young local gang members boarded the train. The German passengers left to go to another car.

The hoodlums approached Charlie and his friend and, in broken English, said, "Give us your things or we'll rape you."

Charlie froze, and his friend tried to hit them. When they started scuffling, one of them hit Charlie's friend in the head, and another one pulled a knife.

Charlie started talking fast, saying, "If you take this stuff now, you'll be seen because obviously there are video cameras on the train. Look, why don't you stand here, and I'll give you my wallet and all my stuff as soon as the train stops, and you can take off."

When the train stopped, Charlie gave the hoodlum his Pepsi to hold while he got his wallet out. Then Charlie led his friend to jump over the seats and bolt out the door and run. There was no way the hoodlums could have caught them.

After returning to Coronado, Charlie spent the next several months preparing to go to BUD/S. (After he made the SEAL Team, he told me how unprepared the new "White Shirts," or newbies, were when they entered the program.)

Most guys thought they were in good shape. They wanted to be a SEAL, and had told all their friends they would be a SEAL. Now they were in BUD/S, so basically they figured they were SEALs.

Big mistake! These men fell out during INDOC (Indoctrination) ... this was before you started BUD/S, to ready the men for what was to come. The next mistake most of the guys made, according to Charlie, was thinking that once you pass Hell Week and earn a brown shirt, you've made it. Out of 365 guys at the start of Class 266, *most* dropped out or didn't make the requirements *after* Hell Week. Pool Comp (Compilation) followed Hell Week, and if the candidate was not comfortable in the water, he was out.

Some of the ways Charlie prepared, besides being fit, was to make the right friends before he started INDOC. He hung around Coronado and met with veterans, both current and former SEALs who had already completed BUD/S training. He met a former SEAL in a bar. They became friends, and he tutored Charlie by teaching him things he would have to do to successfully complete SEAL training. They became lifelong friends.

C4 made another lifelong friend, who was just ahead of him in the SEAL training. He gave him all kinds of help in learning to overcome the hardships of each phase of BUD/S before he got there.

He took Charlie to a swimming pool, where Charlie was tied up and, underwater, had to free himself—one of the tasks they knew he would have to do. Of course, this was dangerous and shouldn't be done without supervision.

Charlie also practiced shooting at the range and running in boots and pants through cold water and sand.

The Navy recruiters told him of Navy obstacle courses where he could practice. He was able to access the SEAL obstacle course in Coronado and continued to run it, and became an expert at it.

Watching The Discovery Channel's *Navy SEALs: BUD/S Class 234* was a tremendous advantage. This was filmed in 2000, when Charlie was in the eighth grade. It's a six-hour series that follows 80 candidates of Class 234 as they try to become SEALs. Each class has a number. The smaller the number, the older the class. Charlie's class would be 266.

The tutorial is great for someone who has aspirations to become a SEAL. Prospective SEAL candidates see the step-by-step type of training they would have to endure and accomplish. Charlie watched this over 50—yes, fifty—times to make sure he knew what to expect. Ron and I watched it almost as many times, in conjunction with what Charlie was doing while he was, in fact, in BUD/S.

Looking back, I believe the *BUD/S Class 234* documentary and 9/11 solidified Charlie's desire to be a SEAL. The best advantage Charlie had was his mental toughness. He wanted to be a SEAL, no matter what. He was not going to quit.

Jeremy showing Charlie how to use
an Apple computer for college.

Charlie in his Indiana University dorm room
with mom, who was pregnant with Ali.

Running for Indiana. *Photo by*
Pete Reinstein. Used with permission.

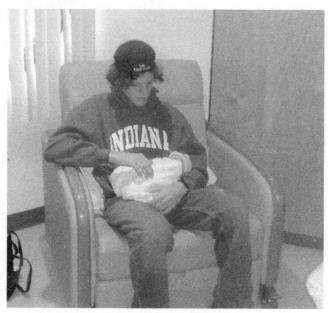

Charlie holding his new sister,
Ali, on the day she was born in 2004.

Pictures with Ali and the
love Charlie always
showed her.

Mom and Ron watching Charlie in BUD/S.

BUD/S Graduation and love when he
dances with mom!

Free time to show mom around.

The favorite day of my life, family fun
in Coronado, California.

Charlie fulfills his lifelong dream of becoming a US Navy SEAL, in June 2008.

Charlie with his homemade Christmas
stocking he used for years.

Being "tough." Charlie, left, with teammate and friend, Pat Feeks. *Photo by Emily Feeks. Used with permission.*

Pre-deployment visits with Ron and Ali close by in
Ponte Vedra Beach, Florida.

Charlie writing the note cards for his speech at the
Department of Environmental Protection Agency,
Jacksonville, Florida, December 23, 2015.

Fun with Ali for her birthday at
Universal Studios in Orlando, Florida.

Charlie visiting his grandparents, my parents, Phyllis and Bill
Holmes, in Phoenix before his last deployment.

Visiting in Rome, at the time, Mother Teresa of Calcutta,
now Saint Teresa.

US Army General Grange (Retired), center; The Lazarus Project,
dedication of the Freedom Bell to Honor US Navy SEAL Charlie
Keating IV, killed in action while rendering support to Kurdish
forces in a firefight against ISIS in the town of Teleskof, Kurdistan.
Photo by Jack Scalia. Used with permission.

My mother, Phyllis Holmes, and I working on our children's books about Charlie. She is the illustrator.

Chapter 14

Becoming a SEAL

According to the SEAL website, the Basic Underwater Demolition/SEAL training is a six-month training course held at the Naval Special Warfare Training Center in Coronado, California. It starts with five weeks of indoctrination and pre-training, as part of a Navy SEAL class, and subsequently goes through the three phases of BUD/S.

The first phase is the toughest, physically. It consists of eight weeks of basic conditioning which peaks with Hell Week at the midway point, when trainees are tested to their limits. It is expected that approximately two-thirds of the trainees will drop out before the end of Hell Week. The miserable wet cold, approaching hypothermia, will make some quit. Sheer fatigue and sleep deprivation will cause others to leave the program.

This is followed by eight weeks of diving and nine weeks of land warfare. During these phases, other SEAL candidates will drop out, usually due to academic issues, demolition safety, or competency issues. Three weeks of basic parachute training follow these phases. After they make it through BUD/S, the next phase is SQT (SEAL Qualification Training). The soldier can be dropped at any time, even in the first year of deployment with the SEAL Team. Getting dropped can be due to mistakes, safety violations, injury, or not getting along with teammates.

Charlie reported to INDOC and received his white shirt. At INDOC, they try to get the soldiers up to speed, fitness-wise.

They get them running and doing push-ups and pull-ups, and paperwork, and some verbal pushing to see if they are tough enough. Charlie had just finished boot camp at Great Lakes in Illinois. The cool thing the Navy started at boot camp was to put the prospective SEALs in a group. They would do extra work-outs and build camaraderie among themselves for their pending BUD/S commitments. It worked pretty well; several in Charlie's group did eventually make the SEAL Teams.

At this point, Ron and I, with Ali, rented an apartment on the top floor, corner, overlooking the Naval Special Warfare Center on the beach where they conducted much of the SEAL training. Ron had recently broken his back paragliding and had a month off while he was in a body cast, recuperating. We had a bird's-eye view of BUD/S Class 266.

We would stand on the beach at five thirty or six o'clock in the morning and watch for the recruits in their white shirts, boots, and camouflage pants, run by the Hotel del Coronado in the morning fog, trailed by a car or truck with a bell. They had to run in and out of the water and roll over the sand to get wet and sandy, becoming a "sugar cookie," and keep up with the group. We wrote messages in the sand, like "Don't give up!" or "266 GO!" before they came by. The students ran along the beach, starting with their shirts on, and at the halfway point they'd take them off and throw them in the truck to make sure they ran the whole way.

As they ran by us, we yelled out, "Good going, guys!"

Little Ali yelled, *"Goo,* Charlie!"

Charlie seemed to love the attention—even though he did not want it.

He had told us the names of some of his buddies, and we'd say, "Good going, John!" or "Keep it up, Cale!"

Later, when we met some of these men, they said, "You're Charlie's parents. I hear you yell for me in the morning. Thanks!"

The SEAL tradition is that when a trainee drops out, he drops his helmet next to a brass ship's bell attached to it and rings the bell three times. Any of the men could terminate their SEAL training at any time by ringing the bell. Or, if they failed at something that they had to pass to continue, they had to ring the bell.

No matter what was thrown in his direction, Charlie was *not* going to quit. He was *not* going to fail at a rotation. Most importantly, he was *not* going to ring the bell.

As they ran, the truck followed them, with someone on a loudspeaker saying, "Ring the bell! Ring the bell! Get out of the pain! Stop working. You can stop anytime you want to. You don't have to do this. You're an idiot! What are you doing this for?"

The candidates typically swam two miles, ran four miles, and then carried Zodiac-type boats on their heads and ran in and out of the waves trying to launch them as a team. This, of course, included the carrying of telephone pole–like logs, elephant runs in the sand, obstacle courses with timed deadlines, and other torturous, inventive ways to either cause the men to quit, or force them into top physical and mental shape. The best advantage Charlie had was his mental toughness. He wanted to be a SEAL, no matter what. He was *not* going to quit.

We'd watch Charlie's class swim miles in front of our condo, after seeing them coming from the "grinder," a big area where the students did pull-ups, push-ups, and lunges while freezing from getting wet and sandy. Everyone on the grinder ended up with a scar on their back from doing so many sit-ups. One of the ways they mentally challenged them was to play a song over and over. Charlie's class heard "Wagon Wheel."

After Charlie became a SEAL, he told me, "Yeah, Mom, we would hear 'Wagon Wheel' over and over. I went to a wedding of one of my Team guys and paid the guitar player $100 to play 'Wagon Wheel' over and over. The bride was not happy." To this day, when I hear "Wagon Wheel," I think of Charlie and, believe me, some of those moments when it plays, I feel like he's sending his love.

The month we spent with Class 266 was one of the greatest experiences of my life. The instructors started to notice us at different locations. We'd hire a babysitter for Ali and find the different challenge locations, and watch from afar. One day we were watching the SEAL trainees as they were returning from a long, difficult swim. They had scuba tanks on and full wetsuits, coming out of the bay under the Coronado Bridge by the park. The instructor noticed us standing along the shore.

When Charlie and his swim buddy came out of the water, the instructor said, "Keating! I'm your parents' babysitter's father. Just for that, drop with your buddy and give me 100 push-ups!"

Charlie and his buddy looked at each other and then at Ron and me. Charlie laughed his big laugh, and they dropped down with their scuba tanks on and knocked out the push-ups. Somehow Charlie loved the challenge, especially in front of his parents!

Another time Charlie and his buddy were standing in the food line toward the front, the instructor noticed the chatter and said, "Hey, if you keep talking, you go to the back of the line."

He cast a glance at Charlie and, grinning, proceeded to the back of the line.

Even though Charlie was one of the best runners, he usually ran near the end of the pack. He'd be encouraging those who were having difficulty keeping up with the pace so they'd get a passing time. We often saw him running alongside a very big SEAL trainee who originally came from Nigeria. This man had to struggle to keep up because of his size. Charlie would drop back and run alongside the man, urging him to keep up.

I said to him, "You're the best runner there. Why the heck aren't you in the front instead of the rear, and show those instructors what you can do?"

He answered, "Mom, you don't want to do anything that makes you stand out. The showoff guy who is in the lead and being a showboat may get rewarded in the end, but the instructors have their eyeballs on him. The minute he does something wrong, they are all over him. You don't want to be that guy. I'm not going to let them know what I can do. Plus, this is how you become a team."

As a result of his preparation and tutoring, Charlie was one of the few SEAL trainees who passed nearly every test on his first attempt in both BUD/S and the follow-on SEAL Qualification Training (SQT). This was important because, for each tested event, any trainee who failed was given only two more tries. If he was unable to complete the task, he was required to "ring the bell" and leave SEAL training. Charlie was known as "first time, every time."

The first two weeks of BUD/S are devoted to physical conditioning to prepare the candidates for Hell Week. During five-and-a-half days of Hell Week, they experience grueling physical training, and the SEAL trainees average about four hours of sleep during the entire period. During this period, they run about 200 miles and spend twenty hours a day running, swimming, or in other physical training.

We found out what day Hell Week would start. The SEAL trainees also knew, but none of us knew what time, although everyone knew it would be at night. Having heard about it, the SEAL trainees were nervous and had been eating as much as they could, and tried to get rest or even a little extra sleep—difficult to accomplish with their demanding schedule.

While most trainees were probably tossing and turning after they went to bed, they knew what was going to happen that night—just not when. As the island of Coronado can testify, over 321 times, explosives and fireworks go off. The residents hear guns shooting and instructors screaming instructions over a bullhorn. There is the clashing of garbage can lids against each other, along with smoke and fire. Trainees were running and hollering out of their bunks, streaking their way toward the beach. Hell Week had started.

I was thinking, *Charlie is running out there.*

I tried to send him a mental message saying, "Okay, Charlie. You have to be able to do this because if you don't make it, you will drop out and will spend your Navy time on a boat somewhere." I knew a Navy ship was way too restrictive for a kid who moved around as much as Charlie.

And, as expected, many of the trainees did drop out, either voluntarily or by failing to complete the required tasks. The unlucky ones might not have made it due to getting hurt or sick during the week. These men were not weak. They had been specifically selected because they were outstanding sailors, physically and mentally capable. At this juncture of their training, though, they were physically and mentally exhausted and only the best of the best could continue their SEAL training.

During Hell Week, the trainees were not able to call or contact us in any way. But I kept in contact with Charlie's friends. They let me know how he was doing.

I'd receive messages like, "He's okay. He looks good. He doesn't have any problems."

But one day, a message from them read: "Charlie's not eating. He can't keep anything down and every time he tries to eat, he vomits and he is clearly losing weight."

It turned out that he had been losing weight throughout the entire phase. The week is a never-ending time of physical activity, freezing weather, swimming in cold water, running miles, and all of this takes its toll on the body. Especially Charlie, who needed a lot of calories to keep his body weight up for energy and warmth.

When he was running races while in school, he found he couldn't eat before a race, or he would vomit. This is not unusual for runners.

When they got their food, Charlie tried to eat but couldn't hold it down. The guys started calling Charlie, "Skeletor." The SEAL instructors were concerned and told him they would "secure" him, which meant he would be given credit for completing Hell Week even though there was a day left.

Charlie refused to leave his Team and continued despite his condition. Later he told us he was hallucinating during the last rotation, called "Around the World." This meant they had to paddle around the island of Coronado at night, during which some of the recruits fell asleep. At one point, while paddling around the island, Charlie thought he saw a low bridge and kept ducking his head to avoid it. Ron and I could see the line of boats with little green lights as they paddled in the dark.

The next day, Charlie and the others who remained in the class were lined up in formation, facing the ocean, waiting to do another tough rotation. They heard the words, "Hell Week is secure!"

When they turned around, the commander and the entire staff were standing at the top of the bank with flags and were cheering for their accomplishment.

So, Charlie had successfully completed the first phase of SEAL training, and the first phase of BUD/S was over. Everyone thinks that completing Hell Week means it's over and you've made it. What they don't know is that Hell Week is only the beginning, and many more candidates drop out in Phase Two, "The Pool."

The men wear white shirts with blue helmets before Hell Week, and the interns are called "White Shirts." After making it through Hell Week they are given the coveted brown shirts and green helmets with their class number, 266, stenciled in white on them. When you see the guys on the beach in Coronado running in brown shirts, you know they made it through Hell Week and are now in the second phase of BUD/S.

After having been denied substantial food for so long, they were adjusting their diets by drinking fruit drinks from small boxes and eating Jell-O.

I was shocked at Charlie's appearance. He was shaking and resembled a skeleton. His cheekbones were sticking out and he had scrapes all over his body, with cuts and gashes on his legs.

The men were given two days off to recuperate before they started the second diving phase of BUD/S. They were justifiably proud of themselves. The men had not only become friends, but also had learned how to work as a team. Further, they had learned how much they could do physically when undergoing unbeliev-able stress and little sleep.

He had to now undergo the second phase of BUD/S, where the students learn combat diving and how to complete long-distance underwater dives.

Of course, Charlie had been swimming since he was two-and-a-half years old and he and his brother had been practicing holding their breath underwater since they were young boys. Charlie also loved to spearfish, which was great for free diving without oxygen. He could hold his breath for three minutes.

With the help of the former SEALs he had befriended, Charlie had practiced some of the more difficult water events they knew he'd be facing. While there is a tendency to panic—and some of the trainees did panic—Charlie was confident and quick-ly freed himself.

Although, as expected, many trainees, unable to complete the various swimming requirements, dropped out in this phase, Charlie again experienced little difficulty, and excelled.

Phase Three is about weapons—running and firing while us-ing different types of pistols, rifles and machine guns. They also learn about explosives. Naturally, Charlie loved the "blowing things up" part. He was assigned as a breacher for his first SEAL Team deployment because he was good at blowing out a door.

Charlie was called "Shaky" by the instructors. Ever since he was a boy, his hands shook with a small tremor. Ron had every-thing checked and medically there was no known reason. Charlie was nervous about pistol shooting because of the shake, yet he overcame this by practicing more. The amazing thing was he lat-er became one of the best snipers on his Team and finished the sniper course at the top of the class. He could stealthily sneak up on anyone.

The men also had to run to the top of a hill with full packs, with extra rocks in them, to a well-known frogman statue. A goal for all graduates was to "touch the frogman" on Frog Hill.

During this time, Charlie also had to float, or "get dirty," in a well of mucky water. He had scratches on his legs still healing from Hell Week, and ended up with MRSA in one leg. MRSA is a bacterial infection that is resistant to many antibiotics and can lead to serious infection or loss of a limb or life. Over the phase, he got to a point where his leg looked like it might have gangrene. Of course, he didn't want to lose his leg. The medic and instructors wanted to helicopter him out and secure him early, but Charlie would not let them. He stayed with his Team, fever and all. He would not let his Team down by quitting early. On his return from the island, Charlie ended up on IVs and constant MRSA medication for another year.

Passing BUD/S was still not the end of the journey. The last part was to pass the SEAL Qualification Training (SQT). BUD/S is intended to weed out candidates. SQT is where the successful graduates learn skills to be successful on deployment.

The final eight weeks of SQT involves mission planning, operations, tactics, and procedures. Only after they had completed every one of these phases would they be awarded the coveted Navy SEAL Trident insignia to wear on their uniforms.

One of the assignments is to go to Alaska in December, when there are only about five-and-a-half hours between sunrise and sunset and the temperatures reach as low as forty degrees below zero.

I was hoping during this time that Charlie would use Ron's "space suit" analogy. During a subzero National cross-country race in Portland, Oregon, he had told Charlie, "You have a space suit on. It is climate controlled. The temperature surrounding your body is neutral." Ron waved his arms around him and said, "It will repel any outside cold and keep you perfectly comfortable." I was happy to hear, on his return, how our trainee indeed used his "space suit."

The candidates are given tactical missions and objectives as they learn how to protect themselves from the elements. They build snow caves, wear cold-weather gear, and learn to use snowshoes while carrying their rucksacks, weapons, and a basic supply of food. They even get into the freezing, icy rivers where they learn how to exit the ice and regain their lost core body temperature.

In one instance, Charlie and the other future SEALs were given a mission in which they had to hike about ten miles, using their compass to find and secure an objective, and set up camp. When they were about halfway to their objective, in freezing sleet, Charlie spotted a deer which was somehow caught on the ledge of a cliff.

From what he told me, Charlie felt sorry for the deer, so he led the group down to the ledge to save the animal. They approached the deer when, while Charlie tried to wrap a rope around it, he almost fell off the cliff. Ultimately, he was able to wrap the rope around the deer, and the group cheered as they were able to slide the deer to apparent safety.

They found, however, that the deer was seriously injured and obviously in a lot of pain. The SEAL chief instructor with the group decided to do the humane thing and shoot the deer. They also learned how to skin and eat the deer for survival.

Later, as the SEAL Qualification Training was ending, the SEAL candidates had a race. The instructors have a tradition of making bets among themselves as to which trainee would win the race.

One of them had an idea that Charlie might be the winner and bet on him. This time, Charlie took off from the start and easily won the race, leaving the rest of the pack far behind. He called me after the race to tell me how excited the instructor who had bet on him was! He also expressed how excited he was to run a race, full out, without worrying about his teammates.

As the SEAL training was coming to an end, some of the instructors told the trainees that before graduation, they should give them gifts in appreciation for the time and effort they had spent on them. Some of the soon-to-be SEALs brought gifts such as a bottle of alcohol, or the video *G.I. Jane*, or a gag gift of some sort.

When they were in the water in the Bay of Coronado, Charlie said, "Watch this!"

He dove under the water with a spear. Shortly after, he came up with a stingray flopping around on the end of his spear and gave it to the instructor.

The instructor was flabbergasted, and said, "I've never had a gift like this before! You've made my day."

Charlie and his remaining classmates were awarded their coveted Navy SEAL Tridents on June 20, 2008. This was my proudest day of my son Charlie because I never thought, when he was seven years old and putting a Navy SEAL poster on his wall, that he would one day really be a SEAL.

Chapter 15

The Deployments

After Charlie's graduation, Ron had the largest bar bill of his life—after buying each graduate multiple tequila shots.

Each new SEAL can request to which side of the country he'd prefer to be assigned. Teams 1, 3, 5, and 7 live in Coronado, and Teams 2, 4, and 10 live on the East Coast, mostly Virginia Beach. Charlie loved Coronado and, luckily, he became a member of SEAL Team 3.

When I visited Charlie, he showed me around his new base. I felt so lucky to be his mom. He showed me the grinder, the bell, the *O* course (*O* for obstacle), the pull-up bar, the room with the class gifts and awards for the SEALs, and, lastly, he showed me the room with glass cases. I say glass cases because it's something you don't want. The 8-foot by 4-foot glass cases contain the boots, gun, helmet, personal items, armored vest of one of the fallen members of SEAL Team 3. They were warriors who were given the Navy Cross or the Medal of Honor for their exceptional service to our country.

Charlie showed me how proud he was of Michael A. Monsoor, who saved the life of other Team members by throwing himself over a live grenade in Iraq, 2006.

I told him, "Good thing there is not enough room for another case in this room!" and winked at my son.

Of course, Charlie subsequently finished his service with SEAL Team 1, and now has his own glass case.

He also showed me where he was not allowed to visit during his training, Danny's and McP's. Now, if you have ever been to Coronado, you know these are the two bars the SEALs frequent. If you are not a SEAL but are in training, *you cannot go in*. If the trainees go in and their instructor happens to be there, they will never hear the end of it and it could also be the end of their time in BUD/S. We visited Danny's for the first time, and Charlie showed me the wall of the fallen SEALs.

"Mom, you don't want to be on that wall," he proclaimed.

Sure enough, when his brother tried to put Charlie's picture on the wall after his funeral, it kept popping off. Not only once, but several times—even hitting a girl on top of her head!

Charlie's first deployment was a four-week orientation tour in Iraq, 2008. During this period, new SEALs were exposed to Iraq in a relatively safe situation. The more senior SEALs used the opportunity to lighten their load by requiring the new SEALs to do some of the menial day-to-day housekeeping tasks, and the newbies learned how to become part of the Team. At the same time, they were learning about Iraqi customs, meeting and inter-acting with the local people, and developing a sense of what it was like to live and work with people in a different culture.

One of the more senior SEALs was Chris Kyle, who later published his best-seller book, *American Sniper: The Autobiography of the Most Lethal Sniper in U.S. Military History*. Chris Kyle became a mentor to Charlie during the first tour of duty in Iraq. Chris Kyle was honorably discharged from the Navy in 2009. Tragically, he was murdered by a former Marine with PTSD at a shooting range on February 2, 2013. As noted in *American Sniper*, there was a reference by Kyle about newbies. Charlie told me he was that newbie whose hair was shaved from his head and glued to his bare chest.

They did a lot of grunt work, as well, as assessed by the new Team members. Grunt work such as guarding all night, cleaning equipment, or whatever the Chief wanted. The most important thing Charlie had to remember was that you can get dropped even as a SEAL, in the first two years of being one. If you don't fit in and you don't measure up to SEAL standards while deployed, you're gone.

Charlie was also introduced to death—of a friend and teammate. Brendan J. Looney was killed on deployment with SEAL Team 3. He was in a helicopter crash in Afghanistan. Charlie went back to Washington, DC, to be at his funeral in Arlington National Cemetery. When the Teams lose a warrior, they help the family as much as possible. They will keep in contact with his family for the rest of their lives, in one way or another. They are part of a large SEAL family. Charlie wore a silver bracelet in his honor.

After Brendan Looney's funeral, the SEALs who attended went to a bar in Georgetown, to mourn their comrade. There was a lot of drinking and before long, a fight erupted between the SEALs and some Naval Academy midshipmen.

The police were called, and some of the SEALs dispersed. One of them ran out and dove into the Potomac River, where he hid under a bridge for hours, using his SEAL skills to stay out of sight.

Meanwhile, Charlie and one of his SEAL friends stayed to try to talk their way out of their predicament. Suddenly, a policeman pulled out his handcuffs and handcuffed Charlie's friend. Charlie took off, running through streets and alleys, chased by another young policeman. When Charlie came to a barbed-wire fence, he again relied on his steeplechase training and vaulted over the fence. This time he wasn't as successful and cut his hand badly, and the policeman caught him.

Charlie started talking: "We were at our SEAL buddy's funeral! We are all upset and trying to pay tribute to him."

The police knew about the ceremony and relented. "Well, you are Navy SEALs and were part of the Arlington ceremony. Sir, be on your way. If anyone presses charges against you, we'll get back to you."

Of course, the Navy midshipmen would have gotten into

trouble too, so no charges were ever brought up.

Charlie flew to Florida, where we lived before he left on his second deployment to Iraq. I was always a bit nervous before he left, although I knew he was well-trained and competent. It's constantly in the back of your mind that something might happen to your child. I didn't go to Coronado, the SEAL base, to say goodbye because I felt I would have a hard time letting go, and perhaps a panic attack when I was boarding the plane for the ride back to Florida.

Instead, Charlie visited us in Florida before he deployed. I loved looking for him when picking him up at the airport. He'd be standing, with a goofy grin, and his rucksack over his shoulder, giving me that small wave I was expecting. Once he'd settled down in the car, he'd start talking. That reminded me of when he'd come home from school and I'd be cooking dinner. He stood and talked about everything, on and on, until his fingers reached into the half-cooked hot hamburger meat and he'd pop some into his mouth and continue talking. (If you knew Charlie, you have seen this over and over.)

Charlie and I had a run together that I will never forget. He was about to deploy to Iraq for the second time, 2010.

I asked, "Charlie, when are you going to get married? Are you going to stay in the SEALs?"

"Mom, I have so much I want to do in my life that I'm not ready to stay in one place." He added, "I would love to live on a boat and sail around the world. I want to make rank as Chief in the SEALs. I'd like to try for SEAL Team 6 and I wouldn't mind instructing in Australia, for their Teams."

I realized he had so many plans; I would not want to keep him from the life he wanted.

I replied, "Charlie, I am so proud of you, and you will find your way, you always do! Marriage and family will be there when you're ready."

A few days later, after running together, talking together, and diving with manatees together in Florida, he left. As he drove away, I wanted him to turn for a final goodbye look, which he did.

Even when Charlie was a little boy, I was able to make a mental connection with him. I could be in the back of an auditorium where Charlie was in a choral performance. I'd be sitting somewhere in a crowd and think, *Charlie, I'm over here.* Within seconds, he'd find me and our eyes would meet.

Another time, when we were skiing, I was on a chairlift and saw Charlie skiing below. I focused on him and thought, *Up here, Charlie. I'm right here.* Sure enough, he looked up and waved to me.

I tried this with my other children and, while it sometimes worked, I always felt truly connected with Charlie. So, as he left this time, I was pleased that once again I had been able to make that mental connection.

When his Team arrived in Iraq, they were camping near a village and quickly made friends with the villagers, who often brought them some of the local goodies as treats. Charlie enjoyed these relationships, especially with the children and their families. I sent packages to him with gum, kids' toys, and cards that he could give the children.

The Team's mission was to help train local Iraqi soldiers and to find traders in the village who were illegally selling weapons and materials to make improvised explosive devices (IEDs). They'd go into a home, search it, identify the illegal trader, and take him into custody. In the end, they usually got the man they were searching for and confiscated a ton of weapons.

When his Team, SEAL Team 3, returned, Charlie and two of his SEAL friends, came to visit us in Crystal River, Florida. They were good friends because of being together during deployment.

Earlier, when we first moved to Crystal River in 2007, I heard there was a family on the same block that had a son in BUD/S SEAL training. Their son was a class or two ahead of Charlie, who was about to start BUD/S training. They met and became good friends, maintaining contact although they were on different SEAL Teams. I became best friends with his mother and this became so stabilizing for both of us when our sons deployed to different locations. To this day, we still have Christmas dinner with their family.

Ron, Adele, Ali, and I were excited to have the three SEALs visit us at home. It was fun to meet such tough-looking guys. Charlie, to us, was still a skinny goofball, but these guys were obviously more experienced at being SEALs; they had been in the Teams longer. Wherever we went, you could see them continually scanning the room and doorways. I felt safe knowing they were with us, even though there was no need to worry. It was kind of a secret, because no one in town knew of their skills, expertise, and vigilance.

While they were with us, we arranged for a man named Kyle (not Chris Kyle the SEAL) to take us out on a boat to go fishing. We caught a lot of fish, and then saw a school of tarpon nearby.

Kyle said, "You can take one of the fish you caught and use it for bait, and try to catch the tarpon. It's amazing!"

The SEALs, of course, wanted to try this and did as Kyle had suggested. This led us to a scene that none of us will ever forget.

Soon a large tarpon latched onto Charlie's bait and put on a show, soaring through the air, and broke free. The baitfish came off the hook and went flying out of the tarpon's mouth. An osprey swooped down, grabbed the fish, and started to fly off, when, out of nowhere, an eagle dive-bombed the osprey. The osprey dropped the fish about three feet from the boat. The eagle swooped down right in front of us and picked up the fish while the osprey, mad as hell, was screeching at the eagle. We gaped at one another, speechless.

Another incident was a bit scary. The SEALs decided to go wakeboarding, which might be compared to snowboarding on water, behind the boat. Each one had to try to outdo the other. As they rode the wakeboards over the boat's wake, they flew into the air and tried to perform acrobatics.

Charlie started off, trying to jump the waves and spin around.

When it came to one of his teammate's turn, he said, "I'm going to do it. Watch this."

He jumped onto the board, started to do a trick—maybe showing off a little for pretty, twenty-one-year-old Adele's benefit—and fell, slamming his ear on the water, rupturing his eardrum. He had just finished a long deployment without getting hurt, and before he got home, he broke an eardrum!

The next time we had another visitor, we had a similar experience. Adele was there, and this man also smashed his eardrum showing off on the wakeboard. Our family joke is that Adele breaks men's eardrums.

Charlie's third deployment was in Afghanistan, 2012. His tour started quietly in the area where he was stationed. While they were productive working with the local people, he wanted some combat experience. If someone was needed to go to Helmand Province, where there was much more action, Charlie would volunteer to be the sniper.

Charlie and his friend, a member of his Team, always worked together, with Charlie as sniper and his teammate as machine gunner. They made a good team, and each had full confidence in the other and backed each other up.

The situation in Helmand, while exciting, was also dangerous. One day their unit was faced with a sharpshooter enemy sniper, and Charlie's job was to take the man out. Charlie was behind a wall, shooting at the enemy when, suddenly, he felt a bullet whip by his head and lodge into the wall behind him.

Luckily the machine gunner returned fire and killed the enemy sniper.

Shortly after that incident, on January 9, 2012, Charlie sat down in Afghanistan to write his sister, Ali, a letter. I would not find out about this until the darkest moment of my life.

In August 2012, Charlie again was going to be a sniper, riding in a helicopter to a remote area in Helmand Province in Afghanistan.

His good friend, Pat Feeks, also wanted to go, so Charlie

said, "You go ahead. I'll go next time."

Pat and Charlie met for the first time in Afghanistan and became immediate friends. They both had the same sense of humor and were raised similarly. Pat was an exceptional athlete as a child. He was an avid bicyclist. Like Charlie, Pat had always wanted to be a Navy SEAL.

The helicopter crashed during a firefight, and all seven Americans and four Afghan soldiers aboard were killed.

Charlie escorted Pat Feeks's body back to the United States for burial at Arlington National Cemetery.

Both Ron, Charlie's girlfriend, and I noticed that Charlie changed after Pat died. He was not as carefree as he had been. He was more thoughtful. It didn't scare him, but it was as though he realized that he, too, could get killed. His combat experiences also triggered unexpected reactions. If there was a Coke can in the road, he would swerve around it like it might be an IED. He was still Charlie, but he was more mature and he had been affected by his experiences. Charlie definitely was a changed man—not in a bad way, but in an "I'm going to live every moment and pay attention way." From that day on, he wore a bracelet in remembrance of Pat.

At the end of the deployment, the SEAL Team members have a break as they are on their way back to the United States. Charlie and his teammates and the helicopter pilots went out on the town in Turkey. He told me he doesn't remember it well, but because the helicopter pilots mean so much to the Teams, he let them tattoo his leg with a message. Unfortunately, something was lost in the translation and no one knows what it says! I'm not a big tattoo person, but Charlie said, with a big grin and hardy laugh, "The pilots are the most important part of our successful missions."

After returning from that deployment and with the death of his close friend and teammate, Charlie decided in 2013 to transfer to Naval Special Warfare (NSW) where, as a Petty Officer, he taught Sniper/Reconnaissance Cell. He would train all the

West Coast–based NSW snipers. After a two-year assignment, he would join his old Team or a new Team.

During another one of our runs, I asked Charlie what he'd like to do in the future. He said he wanted to stay in the SEALs. This new assignment would keep him moving up in the ranks. He really wanted to make 'Chief', which he did posthumously.

When he finished the two-year assignment, he joined SEAL Team 1 as the leader of his platoon.

Chapter 16

The Last Visit

On December 22, 2015, Charlie and his fiancée, Brooke, came to visit us for his little sister, Ali's, birthday and the Christmas holiday. This was the first time I had met Brooke. Right away, I liked her, even though there was not much time to get to know her, and Charlie and Brooke were at the start of a much-needed long vacation. This was also Charlie's pre-deployment vacation before he left for Iraq in February. Although I didn't realize it then, I now consider this their honeymoon.

I knew they were going to get engaged because while speaking to him on the phone earlier, I asked him, "Is this the one?"

He enthusiastically said, "Yes!"—which was so much out of character for him.

While at our house over Christmas, they decided on the date for the wedding as November 12, 2016, after he'd return from deployment. Charlie was showing Brooke around the house and he stopped at the bird, Doc. Doc was purchased when Charlie was in middle school because he "wanted a bird that could talk." Doc is an African grey parrot who talks, but due to him having been abused earlier in his life, he won't let anyone hold him. He bites everyone and everything; however, he speaks in everyone's voices.

Charlie went up to the cage and started screeching, "Caw, caw, caw," over and over. Even though he was thirty, he still acted fifteen.

"Charlie, stop doing that," I begged. "The bird will repeat it over and over when you leave. Please … stop."

Now, instead of being angry, I smile because to this day Doc is doing that over and over in Charlie's voice.

While they were visiting, I also mentioned, "Well, you might want to get married before you leave and don't tell anyone. You can still have a formal wedding in November after you return. That way, Brooke would be included with the wives' support groups of married SEALs who are deployed."

Ron and I and Charlie and Brooke took Ali to Universal Studios in Orlando for her birthday. We had a great time. Not only was Ali excited to visit The Wizarding World of Harry Potter, but Charlie let her pick out her own wand. He went on every ride with Ali, including the Rock 'n' Roller Coaster, a thrilling ride in a simulated limousine, all done to the music of Aerosmith. Charlie let Ali choose the Aerosmith songs as they sped along in the roller coaster. The photos they shared with us later showed Charlie with his arm around his little sister and demonstrated the special bond between the two.

When I reminisce, viewing pictures of our family, I notice that in every single one he has his arm around Ali or she is on his shoulders or he is sitting next to her. The picture of them walking hand in hand on her birthday, at Universal Studios Florida, is my favorite. Brooke caught that moment.

Ali's birthday is right before Christmas. After she was born, she had a medical problem and wasn't able to leave the hospital until Christmas Eve. So, when our kids visit for Christmas, they include her birthday, which is on the twenty-second.

The last Christmas with Charlie surprised me. While we were opening gifts, I said, "Charlie, I'm so glad you're with me for Christmas!"

He said, "Mom, don't you realize I'm always with you on Christmas?"

I felt like an idiot. I recalled all the Christmas days he was not deployed, and there he was, opening his handmade stocking from Santa with the "ie" missing from his name and the two-dollar bill still in the front pocket. I felt horrible I hadn't noticed that small thing that he felt so deeply. I feel even worse about it now.

During his visit, I said, "Charlie, a lot of the SEALs do speaking engagements. I have someone here in Florida who would love to have you speak at their holiday party. The topic is teamwork. You can get some experience and see how it goes."

"Mom, the SEALs don't like to advertise. I don't want to let too many people know what I do. The guys out there writing books are giving away secrets that put our Teams in jeopardy."

I said, "This is about teamwork, and I would love to see you speak and hear a little about you guiding your new platoon for this deployment to Iraq. My parents, Brooke, and Ali will be there, and we won't say a word, and the company promised not to take pictures or give out your information." I added, "It would be good practice for you."

Little did I know at the time, this was a gift from God.

Charlie was introduced to the Florida Department of Environmental Protection Agency in Jacksonville, Florida, on December 23, 2015. About sixty employees attended. Charlie walked into the room in flip-flops, a Hawaiian shirt, and floppy hair. I was hoping for a uniform, but he and Brooke were off on their pre-deployment vacation the next week.

Actually, the whole room was caught off guard, including their leader. He asked the room what they thought Charlie was going to speak about. He had a little grin on his face and looked around the room.

The night before, I had watched Charlie organize his note cards, and remembered his speaking in high school when he did the same thing.

On stage, Charlie held about ten cards in his left hand. The room was loud and people were conversing to the person seated next to them. No one was hearing what their leader was saying.

As they turned their attention to him, he said, *"US Navy SEAL."*

The room went silent. Charlie smiled at them, loving the attendees' surprise.

After Charlie told them his name, the question he asked was: "Is there anyone in the room in the military or who has been in the military?"

Several men and women raised their hands. He had broken the silence and asked each one what they did and thanked them for their service. Charlie was the ultimate gentleman and, at that moment, a leader. I was proud of my son.

He first told them about his life growing up and how he became a SEAL. He spoke of his running career and swimming. He also said that traveling was a big influence and having a sense of adventure. He explained that BUD/S either brings the best out of you or the worst out of you.

He said that when he was in Hell Week, he didn't say to himself, "So I've got to get all the way through to Saturday." If it was morning, his goal was to simply make it to lunch, and "by doing this, you obtain a small goal and then reward yourself with a pat on the back. Set the next goal of making it to dinner, and so on."

The most important comment he made, however, was about his SEAL Team.

He said, "As a team, you need to overcome your challenges." He added, "No matter how small or insignificant the task, doing your best is the way to go. Find a deeper meaning in menial tasks and remember that every action affects the bigger picture."

He used personal examples of "Staying positive and calming down in a stressful environment" and related them to the room. He showed them how to correct a wrong call or decision and make it work to your advantage.

He pointed out that he wasn't a screamer, and would look for the good things his Team members did and recognize them for those achievements. Doing this would be motivating by building them up.

He added, "The most important lesson is to have respect for all people. Everyone has something to share, regardless of their age, rank, or background. The newest guy will always teach you something new. Nobody in my platoon ever says, 'That's not my job!'"

Charlie said, "I have to be good at multitasking when bullets are flying by and my earpiece is telling me something else. It helps to stay focused and cool under pressure." He liked to align himself with the people who shared that work ethic.

He closed by saying, "Be passionate about your job, no matter what it is. You are always respected if you're passionate. And lastly, always have your buddy's back, whether it's at work or in your personal life."

The room erupted into clapping and the attendees asked many questions. After he finished, he was mobbed with personal stories. I watched him patiently listening to them. I saw my son in a different light and knew I had just witnessed perfection.

As we walked out of the building, Charlie had the note cards in his hand. He started to throw them into a trash can, when I noticed and asked him for them. Another miracle. I took them and put them in my purse, silently hoping he would come back safely. To this day, if anyone stole my purse, I would not miss my wallet or credit cards—I would miss those note cards, still in my purse from that day.

On a sympathy card, an employee wrote to me: "It was an honor to hear Charlie speak and shake his hand. I will always remember him, his dedication to his team, and his enthusiasm for life. Thank you for sharing him with us."

Another employee wrote, "I was very shocked and saddened to learn of Charlie's passing. He made a big impression on many of us when he came to speak. Learning the news reminded us of how small the world is ... and the profound connection we can have with someone we only meet once. I am very grateful to have seen Charlie speak and was inspired by his words."

An employee who wasn't in the room stated, " I was, however, able to overhear bits and pieces and when I heard Charlie refer to 'having a passion for everything you do and that no task is too small or insignificant, always bring your best,' it really made me smile and proud to be part of this team and doing what I needed to. We are blessed to have met him. He is an inspiration."

I realize those staff members that Charlie spoke to have had a hard time since his death. Within five months they would hear the news. I hope they see that allowing his family the opportunity to hear what he did and how he was the leader of his platoon was a gift to us and "thank you."

PART III

'I Will Always Be with You'

Chapter 17

Faith

When Charlie was a small boy, we were fortunate enough to visit Rome and be able to meet with Mother Teresa, who is now a saint.

We came to an area of old Roman buildings, some offices, and some homes. We entered a small, nondescript church with open windows on a warm, sunny day. The church was clean, with a floor of part dirt and part concrete. There was a statue of the Virgin Mary, a cross in the front, and some wooden benches and kneelers. A blackboard on the left side had a numbered column. It was a list. I examined it more closely.

Number one was "Conversion of Russia." Number two was "Conversion of China." The third was "Abortion." Fourth, "Unite Germany." These were things the nuns who were present were supposed to pray for and it was their only job.

At the time, I thought, *How is that going to happen? Just sit here and pray?*

Later, the Berlin Wall came down, uniting Germany; the Union of Soviet Socialist Republics (USSR) dissolved; and huge strides have been made with the right to life. The power of prayer!

We were watching the nuns, when one of Mother Teresa's assistants came and said, "Mother Teresa is coming!"

When she walked through the doorway, she went directly to the children. A nun picked Charlie out of my arms and handed him to Mother Teresa, and I started taking photographs.

Now that Mother Teresa is a saint, I try to remember details about her. She was small, and I had to bend over to hear what she was saying. She seemed fragile yet strong. She spoke very clear English. She kissed a Virgin Mary medal and gave it to us. I framed it and hung it on the wall in Charlie's room. The last thing I remember about her is what she whispered in my ear: "Be one with Christ."

I was raised in the Lutheran religion. There was no pressure on me to become Catholic. I did, however, feel it was important to raise children in the same religion as their parents. I met a wonderful priest, Father Frank Fernandez, and went to him for counseling.

I asked a million questions, such as: "Why is the Virgin Mary so important? Why do you kneel in church? Why is the cross everywhere? Why do Catholics make the sign of the cross? Why are there saints? Why are there so many statues? What is a mortal sin? Why do you have to go to confession?"

The answers Father Fernandez gave me were logical, and I started to realize that faith was about believing in something bigger than yourself. Knowing there is a God. Feeling that there is a God. Becoming Catholic was important to me and wanting to raise my children in the Catholic faith was important to me. The Catholic faith was important to my son, Charlie.

Our Navy SEAL didn't share his thoughts about faith before deployment. I saw it in his eyes. He was confident and knew he was doing the right thing. Charlie believed he was saving the world from evil. His favorite books growing up were *The Lord of the Rings* and the Harry Potter series, and his favorite movies were *Star Wars* and, of course, *Rambo*, with good versus evil, and good always won.

I was reminded of these lessons of faith and Charlie's combat accomplishments as we followed the hearse in his funeral procession. We started at the Catholic church on Coronado Island and proceeded to Fort Rosecrans National Cemetery in Point Loma. We were led by more than 100 Patriot Guard riders on their Harleys, or "hogs." They are men and women on motorcycles with flags, who lead veterans' funeral processions. It was stunning and loud.

The streets were lined four rows deep of families, children with flags, veterans in salute, fire trucks with a veil of flags that went on for miles. As we drove onto the freeway, Jeremy noticed on his phone that Fox News was showing the procession live from a news helicopter. I watched the scene from above and realized the enormity of my Charlie's death. Ahead, on the freeway, it was almost empty. Cars were pulled off to the side. I saw one woman jump out of her car, crying, "Thank you." … It was very sad, but so incredible for my son.

Finally, as we rounded the corner to proceed up the steep incline to Rosecrans Cemetery, families were lining the road the whole way, waving another country's flag. I wondered what country they were from. The entire half-mile was lined with them. Then it dawned on me; they were Iraqi families waving their flag. I was floored and so proud of my son that people from another country were thankful for his life.

The biggest blessing, as a mother, is to know your son had faith. I watched him go to church every Sunday and saw my son kneel and pray to the greater glory of God. I heard stories of how he helped save his teammates and the villagers of another country.

I felt like I lost my faith during the week of his death. I wanted to know if it was worth his life to die for our country. The amazing miracles the day of his funeral ended with a blessing. I was handed the letter he wrote to Ali, from Afghanistan in 2012. Part of that said:

> … Just remember with whatever happens to me
> I will always be with you and I'll be in a much
> happier place. Keep Mom and your Dad strong
> and keep your faith in God.
> Love you lots
> C4

I listened to Charlie, through Ali's letter. I believe Charlie is in a much happier place. I feel it sometimes when finding small white feathers on the beach, hearing "Wagon Wheel" play on the radio, watching an eagle float by, receiving an unexpected message from an old friend about him, and seeing Ali smile just like Charlie. Most of all, the warmth of my heart when thinking about him makes the hole in my heart smaller.

I've read somewhere "that our greatest moments of pain can be our greatest chance to grow in our faith and to share it with others." This is exactly what I have been feeling. I never truly believed this until my son died.

One of the letters I received from a little girl named Valeria Dominguez, a student at the Catholic school on Coronado Island, says it all:

> I don't know if I can console you very much because I haven't endured such a strong loss like you've had. What I do know is that everybody is in search of that one moment that marks our life. For some that moment may be falling in love, going on an adventure, or saving the world from a zombie apocalypse. Throughout my 14 years of my life, my spotlight has been when I was sitting outside a funeral service on a very cloudy day. I know it's odd, my life's boom is in a funeral? I was sitting with my father in the white chairs when I suddenly felt an odd warmth striking my face. It was the sun's ray. I looked directly at the cloudy sky, wondering where the ray had come from. Then I saw it. I was amazed by this small detail! There was a small, perfectly shaped circle forming a rift in between the clouds, from where the sun's ray passed through. For some, my life's spotlight might be silly, but for me it was the best moment of my life! For your heroic son, his spotlight might've been his entire life, every single

second of it! He achieved everyone's dreams! He fell in love, saved people, became a hero, and most importantly: He became an angel! He became your guardian! The beautiful baby boy you held in your arms, the child you cared for, the boy you raised, the man you felt extremely proud of.
Given to me on my first Mother's Day without Charlie, May 2016.

Coping with the loss of a child is hard for other people to imagine. It is your worst nightmare. It doesn't matter how it happened, but what matters is they are not here to call, take care of, or hug. It's not something you "just get over." Every morning of every day you wake up and think about your child. Many mothers I speak to have children who died in other ways. Opioid addiction is the hardest for them. I still feel that Jesus surrounds those who are sick and in pain first. He will be there for them, to escort them to a better place without the continual suffering of their addiction.

The unexpected grace of losing a child is that I now feel closer to God. I can't explain it. I have extremely bad days when I miss Charlie so much. But a parent's role for a child is to help him or her achieve their goals in life. This also means teaching them about our history through the Bible. I wanted so much, as a mother, to have Charlie find a good job, support himself, get married, have a family, be healthy, and enjoy life. What I realize now is that he is in heaven and that was the point of life. He is happy, not hungry, out of pain, and with the glory of God.

I spend my time writing children's books about him and his big heart. I was encouraged by Will Merrill, my coauthor, to complete a book I had started in Charlie's honor. I also worked with my mother, Phyllis Holmes—Charlie's grandma—who was the illustrator. These were times I can't get back or never would have had if Charlie hadn't finished his mission. My mother and I remember how motivated Charlie was as a boy. He was a person who aspired to greatness, and the books represent those stories. Of course, The Big-Hearted Charlie Series isn't about Charlie's sacrifice. The books are to motivate kids and teach them about fortitude and how to be successful.

It's much easier to cope by taking my loss and moving it to a project for others, especially children. Charlie would have liked that.

Ron and I have remained strong ... no, stronger. We both value the moment more. We value time and the life around us. It's easier to let the little things go. We enjoy.

Ali, for her part, is going forward with her swimming and still wondering why we're sad sometimes. She still tells us, "What's the problem? Charlie is in heaven!"

So, as to the last part of Charlie's letter, "Yes, my son, we have kept our faith in God."

Love you lots,
Mom

Chapter 18

Miracles

Charlie started delivering special moments surrounding his Catholic faith.

I received a message from a friend of mine who was in touch with an Iraqi priest in the town of Teleskof, Iraq. The Order of St. Lazarus from the United States sent a church bell to Father Rem for his parish in Iraq.

In his dedication of the bell to the church, Father announced, "The American soldier, Navy SEAL Charles Keating, died right here in this town, on this border where we are standing. Here on this border, his blood was mixed with the blood of the young soldiers from this town who defended the freedom of this town. In Charlie's name, this bell will be placed in the tower of this church behind me. I am praying for his soul. This bell, from now on, will be called the Charles Keating Bell of Freedom."

It is rung every Sunday to call worshippers to Mass.

Another miracle actually happened at the White House. Ron and I were invited to the White House to attend a Gold Star ceremony with President Trump and his wife, Melania, on June 4, 2018. We didn't know how long the ceremony was going to be— if it was going to be five minutes or if it was going to be dinner. So, we guessed it was going to be a half-hour ceremony.

I wore a nice dress with covered shoulders, and nylons (which I never wear), and covered heels. Ron wore his best suit and a nice purple shirt. He never wears a handkerchief in his pocket, but this day he had a handkerchief in his pocket.

We were eager, and ensured an early arrival in case there were any problems with security. It paid off!

We were among the first to arrive and were able to enjoy going through the lower rooms of the White House without a crowd. We viewed china that our forefathers had eaten on, as well as spectacular art. I took some pictures of Ron and me sitting by one of the windows. We could see people peering in and wishing they could join us.

A huge banquet table was covered with a large variety of hors d'oeuvres. We were offered Champagne along with food and spirits. We realized then, we were going to be there for much more than a half-hour.

We decided to bypass the hors d'oeuvres to be sure we'd be present on time to meet the president. I had rehearsed what I was going to say to him, time and time again, the night before. When we arrived, we saw a mixed bag of people. There were Gold Star Families with losses from Vietnam, from World War II, from the Korean War, from Afghanistan, and from Iraq. I will never forget the mother with her three young children, who had lost her husband only months before.

About 150 people represented fifty enlisted men and women who had died in the service of our country. After the president arrived, we got in line to meet him and have our pictures taken.

When we approached the president, I stepped forward and said, "Hi, President Trump. I'm Charlie's mom. Two years ago, when my son was killed, someone from your office called, but I could not talk to them because I was on my way to his memorial service. Later, when I was at a meeting with some Navy SEALs, I asked them what they would tell you if they could. They said, 'Crush Hillary!' 'Crush ISIS!' And you did both!"

The president smiled and replied, "I did both. Yes."

He leaned forward, toward my ear, and whispered, "Frankly, it was harder to crush ISIS."

Then he gave a thumbs-up motion, and the photographer

snapped our picture.

After that, we left and were seated for the ceremony, which began when Melania entered the room. She'd had kidney surgery three weeks earlier, and we thought she appeared a little weak. I could tell she was making a huge effort to be at the ceremony. We were grateful.

Nearly the entire White House Cabinet was present at the ceremony. Also present were Vice President Mike Pence and Mrs. Pence, Chief of Staff General John Kelly, and National Security Advisor John Bolton.

The ceremony was very moving. After we were seated, they lit a candle for each of the men and women who had died. I was overwhelmed. They lit each of the candles and read the name of the person being honored. When they lit the candle for Charlie and read his name, birth, and death dates, I realized it was representing his life. I felt Charlie's presence and, after having held myself together for a long time, I could not hold back the tears. I silently cried.

When the ceremony was over, a woman made a beeline toward me. She had just returned from a visit to Mosul, Iraq. We talked for a couple of minutes and she showed us a photo of a man standing near where Charlie was killed. I wanted to meet her individually and give her copies of the children's books I had written about Charlie, so I made an appointment to meet with her the next morning. I didn't realize at the time that this would become something special.

Ron and I made our way to the West Wing of the White House the following morning. We were met by a White House Fellow and went through security. Everywhere we went, people were pleasant, smiling, and making eye contact with us.

When we reached the woman's office, we were introduced to several top government advisors. After we all sat down, we learned that the group had traveled to tour the status of Mosul and Iraq on the ground. The purpose of the tour was to find out what the United States could do to help stabilize Iraq and help the

Iraqi citizens. They traveled in armored Humvees with officials and an interpreter, north of Mosul.

As the Iraqi tour members talked among themselves, the woman told us she kept hearing the word "Charlie." She didn't think too much of this—until they met a Peshmerga general. Again, they heard "Charlie" mentioned. The general pounded his chest and started to cry, which I found out later is common among Iraqis when mourning.

The American advisor asked the interpreter what they were talking about.

He answered, "The Navy SEAL who gave his life for us."

The advisor was taken aback, repeating this out loud to the rest of the group, of how they kept hearing Charlie's name and how profound that was.

The Peshmerga general said he wanted to show them something, so the group jumped into their vehicles and followed him. He led them to the place where Charlie had died, and pointed out where the sniper had been when he shot my son.

The Iraqi general asked for two things: They wanted to build a chapel where Charlie died and a playground for children.

I was stunned. The two things Charlie loved the most.

Epilogue

I have wanted to share my faith and love of God. It doesn't have to be specifically my Catholic faith, but the faith in your heart when you do something good. The pull to be a better person. It's not only going to church every Sunday, but putting those lessons to use in your life. It is not easy to always be a good person. However, Charlie taught me to try harder.

A few months after Charlie's funeral, I remembered this incident: On the evening of April 18, 2016, after swim practice, a month *before* Charlie's death, Ali was preparing for bed. I was going to feed the dogs, so I went down the steps, into the garage, for the dog food. It was quiet and dark except for a flashing blue light from our invisible fence. In the garage, I immediately felt something strong and pleasant coming from near the left corner. I looked over to see if someone was there. I couldn't see anyone, but I still felt a wonderful feeling of happiness and inner warmth, as though I was in the presence of someone holy.

Feeling afraid at this amazing rush of goodness and the strong feeling in my heart, I ran back into the house. The feeling stopped abruptly.

After a few minutes, I felt I had to go back to see if I was crazy. I returned to the garage.

I felt it again. I cannot explain how wonderful my heart felt. Was it Jesus? Mary? An angel? I felt like it was Mary, Jesus's mother. I felt frightened and wanted to run away. But I didn't want this glorious feeling in my chest to stop. I was embarrassed and felt I didn't deserve what was happening. I stood there as long as I could. Ali was expecting me back for prayers.

I said out loud, "I haven't done a lot of great things. Is there something you want me to do?"

No response. But the feeling was still strong. I worried that if she told me to do something, I might not be able to do what she wanted, so I hesitated, and left the garage. I put Ali to bed and went back. Mary was gone.

I applaud Mary. When visited by an angel asking her to carry the son of God, she said yes. She must have been a brave girl.

I hesitated to tell Ron because I felt he would think I was indeed crazy. I eventually explained to him what had happened.

He replied, "Well, Jesus was born in a manger, why not Mary in our garage."

I married the right man! He loves me enough to believe me.

Maybe the message in the garage was my "life's boom," as the fourteen-year-old Valeria Dominguez wrote in the Mother's Day letter to me.

A friend of mine, Alicia, that I hadn't seen in eight years, also sent me a message:

> At a risk of sounding like a complete fruit-loop … Charlie came to me today while I was meditating. He wouldn't stop talking until I promised him I would give you his message.

That certainly sounded like him. He was persistent and did a lot of talking.

> He wants me to tell you he loves you and thanks you for all you are doing in his memory and that you are doing "amazing things" … and that he lived his time here, and while he misses you, he watches over you all and loves you. He said he was doing well and that he was thankful you were his mom and he told me multiple times how happy and peaceful it was on the other side.

There is nothing in the message that I did not want to hear. I have learned since losing my son that I feel there *is* life after death. There *is* hope for your child. When you lose a child, you feel like you lose hope … what they would have been, what they would have become, what their children would be like. What

I have learned is that by doing something with your loss, you can help others deal with their loss. This can be through starting a foundation, writing, knitting, tutoring, or using any of your God-given talents. In a way, helping others helps me live a more fulfilling and less sad life. If you learn anything from the story of my son, never give up. He wouldn't, and I won't.

Charlie made a difference. He was an extraordinary person and he believed in something greater than himself. He lived that every day. I don't want his legacy to be forgotten. Like so many others, I will always be grateful to have been a part of his life. I also learned that the point of his life is that there really isn't an end if you believe in something greater than yourself and you have faith.

Acknowledgments

From Krista Keating-Joseph:

I want to thank my daughter, Ali Joseph, for allowing me to include the letter Charlie wrote to her. Ali, he will always be with you! I also want to thank my husband, Ron Joseph. He has been patient and supportive for four years while I have been pouring my heart out in writing. Of course, to Charlie, I will run with you again one day.

I also thank my parents, Bill and Phyllis Holmes; Amy Rosewater, for getting me going; and Ed Wilks for making it happen. Thank you also to David Thomas, Amanda Luedeke, Beth Mansbridge, Kelly Valentine, Emily and Ginny Feeks, Jack Scalia, Pete Reinstein, and U.S. Army Veteran CJ Stafford. My thanks also to Coronado's Sacred Heart Catholic Church, and to Valeria Dominguez and all those who provided comments or shared stories and letters.

Most importantly, I thank Will Merrill for helping me write my son's story and preserving his legacy – and for listening to me for three years every week.

Lastly, to my faith in God, it has made a difference in my life.

Services that continue to support our family in a positive way are: U.S. Navy SEALs, The U.S. Navy, The Gold Star Family program, TAPS, The Navy SEAL Foundation, K9s for Warriors, America's Mighty Warriors, and the USO. Thank you!

From Colonel (Retired) Will G. Merrill Jr.:

My thanks to Barbara Merrill, my wife, for her patience during the days and hours I spend writing. Thank you to William Quinn for reviewing and helping edit the first draft.

About the Authors

Krista Keating-Joseph, a Gold Star Mom, is also the author of the Big-Hearted Charlie Series of children's books based on true stories of her fallen Navy SEAL son, Charles Keating IV. The first book in the series, *Big-Hearted Charlie Runs the Mile*, earned the Royal Palm Literary Award from the Florida Writers Association. Krista graduated from the University of Arizona, which she attended on a cross-country scholarship. She has been a nationally ranked runner since age nine. Krista has coached high school cross-country and worked in public relations and healthcare marketing. She coaches running at her daughter Ali's school. She has raised two sons, two daughters, and one stepson.

Krista and her husband, Ron, live in Ponte Vedra Beach, Florida, where she teaches Sunday School at Our Lady Star of the Sea Catholic Church and volunteers for Daughters of the American Revolution, The Jean Ribault Chapter. Krista and Ron enjoy outdoor activities such as paddleboarding, biking, body surfing, running, skiing, and tennis.

Contact the Author
kristakeatingjoseph.com
CharlieDontBeAHero.com

Colonel (Retired) Will G. Merrill Jr. is the author of *9/11 Ordinary People: Extraordinary Heroes*, the chosen book of the year in the Royal Palm Literary Award competition and by militarywriters.com http://militarywriters.com/. His second book, *Ordinary People: Extraordinary Heroes – Afghanistan and Iraq,* was awarded First Place in the History category in the Royal Palm Literary Award competition.

Will is a 1958 graduate of the United States Military Academy and served thirty-one years in the US Army, including duty in Germany, Vietnam, the Korean Demilitarized Zone, and Greece, where he narrowly escaped two assassination plots and survived a helicopter crash. He retired with the rank of colonel. His personal decorations include the Department of Defense Superior Service Award, Legion of Merit, Bronze Star, four Meritorious Service Medals, Army Commendation Medal, and Vietnamese Honor Medal.

Will and his wife, Barbara, live in Ponte Vedra Beach, Florida. They have two sons and two daughters. Their sons graduated from West Point, and one also retired as an Army colonel. One granddaughter also served in the US Army, with tours in Iraq and Afghanistan.

Books by Krista Keating-Joseph

Big-Hearted Charlie Runs the Mile
Big-Hearted Charlie Never Gives Up
Big-Hearted Charlie Learns How to Make Friends
Big-Hearted Charlie's Coloring Book:
The Story of a Dog Named Turtle and a Turtle Named Dog

Books by Colonel (Retired) Will G. Merrill Jr.

9/11 Ordinary People: Extraordinary Heroes
Ordinary People: Extraordinary Heroes – Afghanistan and Iraq

CPSIA information can be obtained
at www.ICGtesting.com
Printed in the USA
LVHW091502250720
661524LV00001B/98